Lauer Series in Rhetoric and Composition

Series Editors, Catherine Hobbs and Patricia Sullivan

Lauer Series in Rhetoric and Composition
Series Editors, Catherine Hobbs and Patricia Sullivan

The Lauer Series in Rhetoric and Composition honors the contributions Janice Lauer Hutton has made to the emergence of Rhetoric and Composition as a disciplinary study. It publishes scholarship that carries on Professor Lauer's varied work in the history of written rhetoric, disciplinarity in composition studies, contemporary pedagogical theory, and written literacy theory and research.

Other Books in the Series

Untenured Faculty as Writing Program Administrators: Institutional Practices and Politics, edited by Debra Frank Dew and Alice Horning (2007)

The Promise and Perils of Writing Program Administration, edited by Theresa Enos and Shane Borrowman (2007)

Networked Process: Dissolving Boundaries of Process and Post-Process, by Helen Foster (2007)

Composing a Community: A History of Writing Across the Curriculum, edited by Susan H. McLeod and Margot Soven (2006)

Historical Studies of Writing Program Administration: Individuals, Communities, and the Formation of a Discipline, edited by Barbara L'Eplattenier and Lisa Mastrangelo (2004).

Rhetorics, Poetics, and Cultures: Refiguring College English Studies (Expanded Edition) by James A. Berlin (2003)

1977

A Cultural Moment in Composition

Brent Henze
Jack Selzer
Wendy Sharer

With
Brian Lehew
Shannon Pennefeather
Martin Schleuse

Parlor Press
West Lafayette, Indiana
www.parlorpress.com

Parlor Press LLC, West Lafayette, Indiana 47906

Printed in the United States of America

S A N: 2 5 4 - 8 8 7 9

Library of Congress Cataloging-in-Publication Data

Henze, Brent.

1977 : a cultural moment in composition / Brent Henze ...[et al.].

p. cm. -- (Lauer series in rhetoric and compostion.)

Includes bibliographical references and index.

ISBN 978-1-60235-041-0 (alk. paper) -- ISBN 978-1-60235-040-3 (pbk. : alk. paper) -- ISBN 978-1-60235-042-7 (adobe ebook)

1. English language--Rhetoric--Study and teaching--Evaluation. 2. Report writing--Study and teaching--Evaluation. I. Title. II. Title: Cultural moment in composition.

PE1404.H399 2007

808'.0420711--dc22

2007047197

Cover design by David Blakesley.
Printed on acid-free paper.

Parlor Press, LLC is an independent publisher of scholarly and trade titles in print and multimedia formats. This book is available in paper, cloth and Adobe eBook formats from Parlor Press on the World Wide Web at http://www.parlorpress.com or through online and brick-and-mortar bookstores. For submission information or to find out about Parlor Press publications, write to Parlor Press, 816 Robinson St., West Lafayette, Indiana, 47906, or e-mail editor@parlorpress.com.

Preface

Looking back at *1977: A Cultural Moment in Composition,* our minds entertained the sticky-soft strains of Debby Boone, the sinister visage of Darth Vader—and a few important questions our readers might have about how we came to and carried out our research for this book. While our "Introduction" provides a scholarly context for this project and explains its position within the larger field of composition studies, here we wish to explain briefly the project's genesis and to reflect a bit on our own positions as researchers and historiographers.

Why Penn State?

This text originated in a graduate seminar that we shared on the history of composition at Penn State University half a dozen years ago. Yet our decision to focus on Penn State's writing program as a way of deepening our engagement with the history of composition was not merely one of convenience. Our primary aims in the seminar were to expand our knowledge of composition history and to gain experience with research methodologies that pay attention to situated practices within that history. We began with the intention that each of us would study the local history of a particular writing program at a different college or university in Pennsylvania and would then produce a series of fairly traditional, individually authored seminar papers. We quickly discovered, though, that these individual endeavors would inevitably be incomplete and superficial because we lacked institutional and collegial familiarity with the programs and people at other schools; we just could not gain adequate familiarity with the histories of various programs in one short semester. Moreover, few of the many sources we needed in order to tell a recent history of writing program development—interviews, memos, handouts, lesson plans, student papers—were preserved in the various university archives. Program records charting institutional responses to open admissions, the "literacy crisis" of the 1970s, the process movement, and other social and scholarly developments were not readily accessible in department or university archives; they were more likely to be found in faculty offices and memories, two areas we would have difficulty accessing as relative strangers.

At Penn State, however, we not only knew the current curriculum and its recent past, but we had already developed working relationships with many of the people who had participated in that past. This institutional and personal familiarity enabled us to access the "hidden" archives—the old file boxes in the attic; the yellowed, hand-written essays in the bottom drawers; the textbooks thankfully overlooked during the last office cleanings; the records of forgotten meetings; and the indispensable memories of departmental personalities upon which this history could be built. As at the other institutions we had considered studying, we were not able to consult finding aids or engage the help of a university archivist, for the records that we sought were not generally archived. But at Penn State we could draw on the extensive memories of our pack-rat colleagues, and these proved to be invaluable resources. In short, we discovered that we could tell the most complex and richest history about composition by focusing on our local site.

As we read more about the history of Penn State during the 1970s and early 1980s, we came to realize the magnitude of Penn State's impact during this era in composition history. The sheer number of students who passed through the writing curriculum at Penn State during this period suggests that the program influenced how composition was—and continues to be—viewed both in the state of Pennsylvania and across the nation. Penn State historian Michael Bezilla explains that the influence of the university's curriculum was far reaching—statewide and nationally—by the mid 1980s:

> One Pennsylvanian in eight who chose to enter college immediately after high school in the 1970s enrolled at University Park or one of the Commonwealth Campuses. More than 110,000 baccalaureate degrees were awarded between 1970 and 1983, along with 21,000 associate and 27,000 graduate degrees. By 1982, one in every thousand college graduates in the United States had earned his or her degree from The Pennsylvania State University.

Many people were influenced by the curriculum at Penn State during this time period—a fact that suggested to us that the history of the Penn State curriculum deserved greater attention.

Additionally, each of us wanted to know—indeed we felt ethically obligated to take up the opportunity to know—the historical conditions that influenced the composition program in which we were participating as teachers and administrators. By writing a collaborative history of our local site, we could work together to understand the multivalent strands—scholarship, culture, politics, economics, personalities, and institutional dynamics to name but a few—that entwined to form the complex and conflicted foundation upon which the current writing program at Penn State was built. We also hoped that this historical investigation might even enable us to see where curricular change was needed. In looking for these areas of change, however, we did not simply look for ways that the program "progressed" to its current state from a flawed past. As Ruth Mirtz, drawing on Robert Connors, warns in her work on the history of writing programs, "our downfall as historians [. . .] is assuming that anything that happened in the past was less effective than what we do in the present and viewing the past as the mistake that the present corrects" (122). Thus, we looked for ways in which the current program might usefully incorporate previous administrative and curricular structures. We asked both "which current program and curricular structures were the result of old battles or outworn tradition?" and "what promising administrative and curricular models from the program's past were lost along the way?"

Our ultimate hope is that the historical details of Penn State's writing program presented here will help other scholars, teachers, and administrators understand the recent past of their own writing curricula. Many of the struggles we recount here have been enacted at many other sites: budgetary constraints, institutional pressure, and personality conflicts are common sources of distress and motivators of change in almost every English department. We therefore offer this study as a point of comparison and contrast for those who are working at other institutions to historicize the development of their local writing programs.

The Challenges of Doing Research at "Home"

Researching one's home department is a tricky business. Yet it is also comforting because it protects the researcher from being lulled into a sense of objectivity—what Donna Haraway has called the "gaze from nowhere" (581). As we gathered files and conducted interviews, the institutional politics and personality conflicts that operate in the daily business of a department became painfully obvious. We discovered the roots of current friendships and professional alliances, and we came to understand the origins of some continuing rifts. Some people were hesitant to discuss issues because they involved other professionals who are still active in the department or in the field. Some of the stories we heard and the historical traces we uncovered were contradictory, and the interpretations of events in the department varied widely. Some of the stories we heard were undoubtedly colored by events of the intervening years or were simply misremembered.

Rather than tidying these disparate, filtered, and embedded traces of the past into a unified story of progress that would make Penn State's current program seem like the culmination of a steady, always admirable, and self reflective path of progress, we have tried to retain the messy traces of these conflicts within our narrative and to highlight how very unpredictable and contingent writing program development can be. To further resist a tensionless tale of progress, we have asked colleagues who were active in composition during the 1970s to read the manuscript and offer responses. Several of these responses are included as sidebars to the text; they offer telling embellishments or counterpoints, "corrections" or alternative views, of the events chronicled in the book. The presence of these sometimes competing voices does not discredit the historical narrative of the text; rather they are integral to it. The history we tell is not seamless, nor is it a tidy tale of "good compositionists and those who oppress them." Rather, it is an  attempt to resist what Mirtz calls the "ahistorical identities and false narratives" that often circulate around the development of writing programs and departmental policies (129).

In compiling this multivocal history, we attempted to uncover as many different perspectives as possible on the writing programs at the time. In addition to attending to archival sources and covering secondary materials—we hope that our indebtedness to previous scholarship is apparent in our notes and commentaries—we gathered a variety of historical traces from administrators (WPAs, writing center administrators, department chairs, directors of undergraduate and graduate studies); program faculty (literature, basic writing, composition/rhetoric, creative writing); and students (undergraduate and graduate). Official documents, such as departmental reports, program memos, syllabi, and catalogues, were perhaps the most obvious choices for study, yet we needed the memories of colleagues to flesh out our work. After all, some of the most significant decisions about how to translate composition theory into classroom practice take place in private office conversations and undocumented discussion. As Barbara L'Eplattenier explains, few histories of writing programs have been told because "administrative negotiation often occurs in conversations in casual settings, outside of the bounds of official meetings; such discussions are not recorded or are only superficially addressed in 'official' documentation" (133). Interviews and correspondence with full and part-time faculty who were active in the department or the field of composition at the time thus served as crucial sources for us.

Despite our best intentions and efforts, some competing voices are undoubtedly missing from this history. As in any historical project, what we found is incomplete. While we ran advertisements in the alumni magazine and scoured the old files opened to us by our colleagues at Penn State, we did not find a wealth of sample undergraduate papers and course syllabi. (We did find some.) We also had difficulty tracking down former graduate students from the late 1970s. Yet we believe the narrative told here, as we explain in further detail in the next chapter, provides an important, localized, and necessarily complex complement to broader histories of composition that have appeared in the recent past.

Acknowledgments

We could not have explored these questions with any degree of success without the help of many colleagues. At the risk of forgetting some of them, we wish to thank them here. Our deepest appreciation goes to three fellow members of the graduate seminar on the history of composition who joined us as co-researchers during the early stages of this project: Brian Lehew, Shannon Pennefeather Gardner, and Martin Schleuse. Their contributions to our conversation about historiography invigorated our thinking about the subject, and traces of their research can still be found in these pages: Brian researched creative writing pedagogies (and interviewed Leonard Rubinstein), Shannon worked in basic writing and writing centers, and Martin researched the state of English studies in the 1970s. We are also grateful to the many people who opened their filing cabinets to us, answered our many questions over email and in person, and helped us locate countless traces of the 1970s: Judd Arnold, Thomas Bayer, Wilma Ebbitt, Richard Leo Enos, Jeanne Fahnestock, Robert Frank, Diane Greenfield, Andrea Lunsford, Edgar Knapp, Martha Kolln, Ellen Knodt, Nancy Lowe, Ron Maxwell, Susan McLeod, John Moore, Douglas Park, Thomas Rogers, S. Leonard Rubinstein, Marie Secor, James Sledd, Tilly Warnock, Harvey Wiener, Tom Wilbur, and Richard Young.

We would also like to thank those who have generously read and given us suggestions on earlier versions of this manuscript, including Sharon Crowley, Lisa Ede, Lester Faigley, Michael Halloran, Janice Lauer, and Richard Young. Thanks to colleagues at our 1999 CCCC presentation whose questions and comments prompted important revisions as we developed the manuscript. David Blakesley also provided valuable suggestions and much needed encouragement. Rosalyn Collings Eves assisted in many ways with the preparation of the final manuscript. Finally, thanks to our sidebar contributors, Hugh Burns, Stephen Bernhardt, Jasper Neel, Janice Lauer, Elaine Maimon, John Warnock, Sharon Crowley, and Lester Faigley, whose voices add vital dimension to this history.

Contents

Sidebars

1977

1 Introduction

Why do people teach composition as they do at any given moment? What determines their choices of textbooks, assignments, and daily classroom activities? Of all the possible approaches to the teaching of writing, why do teachers settle on particular ones? What accounts for the shape of composition programs—sequences of courses, testing and placement procedures, staffing and administrative practices? Individual preferences and personal styles are certainly involved; so, of course, are institutional values and constraints. But even more certainly, the teaching of composition is shaped by the available means of pedagogical persuasion that are presented to us by intellectual and professional communities (broadly considered)—communities shaped, inevitably, by culture, circumstance, and history.

History—that aggregate of options and identities offered to us by the material, intellectual, and cultural circumstances of the past—is centrally involved in choices about pedagogy. Recognizing this, in the past few years many scholars have turned their attention to the history of composition after World War II, probably because the period was responsible for the formation of composition as a scholarly discipline and because many disciplinary conventions formulated between 1945 and 1980 have persisted into current practice. Joseph Harris, for instance, in *A Teaching Subject: Composition Since 1966,* has discussed how five key terms have recently dominated and directed scholarly debates about composition (*growth, voice, process, error, community*). Robert Connors in *Composition-Rhetoric* has included within his broad history of writing instruction in America a study of how successive editions of James McCrimmon's *Writing with a Purpose* reflect changes in writing instruction that occurred between 1950 and 1980. Lester Faigley's *Fragments of Rationality* provides three chapters of a broad history of composition from 1960 to 1990 that is poised against the cultural construct known as postmodernity. Sharon Crowley's *Methodical Memory* and *Composition in the University* detail and critique the development of current-traditional rhetoric and the invention of the universal requirement. And shorter studies of one or another piece of composition history since 1945 have begun to appear as well.[1] Together these efforts have filled in many of the details necessarily omitted from broader surveys of the period like James Berlin's *Rhetoric and Reality: Writing Instruction in American Colleges, 1900–1985* and Susan Miller's *Textual Carnivals.*[2] And together they have done a considerable amount to deepen our understanding of the cultural events and intellectual developments that directed the profession in general as well as particular teachers working in the field during the 1970s—that formative decade in the development of composition studies that is just now "entering history," as it were.

Despite the achievements of these scholarly histories, however, certain problems persist in our collective understanding of composition in the 1970s and in our appreciation of how that period has affected current pedagogical practice. First, the histories have been partial in the sense that they have understandably focused more on one or another particular aspect of composition in the period (e.g., Faigley's attention to the history of the process movement, for instance, or Harris's accounting of just five key terms, or David Russell's history of writing across the curriculum, or Susan Miller's emphasis on the gendered material conditions of composition teachers in this century) and less on recreating a sense of the rich, sometimes conflicting, sometimes even random intellectual and material hurly-burly of the period. Consequently, our field has been left without a sense of how all those individual movements were collectively influencing and impeding composition practices in the 1970s or how they generated competing, conflicting, and cooperating discourses at given moments that continue to resonate today. In addition, histories of composition since 1945 have sometimes represented themselves as linear Grand Narratives. Such narratives are useful, to be sure, for staking out in broad terms the boundaries of and developments in the field, for defining important trends, and for clarifying those developments that have persisted most stubbornly into current practice, but they are somewhat less serviceable for preserving the astonishing range of practices, personalities, and messy particulars that strove for a hearing, however temporarily, within the mixed aggregate that has been known as composition. While it would be a serious exaggeration to claim that the histories we have named have been insufficiently attentive to the broad cultural frames, intellectual currents, and social developments that directed the culture of composition in the 1970s, or inattentive to the range of significant pedagogical practices and institutional concerns current at the time, it nevertheless seems fair to say that, within composition studies, understanding of the era is incomplete, lacking in the rich, competing particulars that defined the period.

Thomas Miller speaks for many, then, when he notes that "without a greater attention to social and institutional history, we cannot achieve the broader goals that have been set by those who have criticized research that treats writing as a decontextualized process" ("Teaching the Histories" 71). Among those "broader goals" are a richer set of pedagogical practices and a greater sense of how the past has shaped current practice. Consequently, we decided to complement those previous studies by looking carefully at the state of composition in one particular year—1977—and to ground our observations in a detailed case study of one specific site—Penn State's University Park campus.[3] That decision to study the developing drama of our field by narrowing sharply what Kenneth Burke would call the "circumference" of the scene under scrutiny has enabled us to discover how and why the field of composition was emerging as an intellectual, pedagogical, and professional practice at a particularly crucial moment.[4] It also has given us an opportunity to recover in great detail—detail that is simply impossible to offer in a broader study—the conflicting and sometimes ephemeral currents that were part of the conversation about composition at a specific time. And this focus has permitted us to look at a host of related literacy initiatives—first-year composition, to be sure, but also professional and technical communication, writing across the curriculum, writing centers, creative writing—that have too frequently been considered separately.

1977 also contributes to the growing body of scholarship on writing program administration. Studies of composition history are just beginning to pay significant attention to the historical development of particular writing programs and to the myriad administrative, institutional, and intellectual conflicts and decisions that shaped those programs. Study of the material traces and archival documents of writing program development, Shirley K. Rose suggests, is a fundamental part of ongoing scholarly efforts to theorize writing program administration. Rich historical detail—preserved through archival materials and the historical narratives assembled from them—"will be useful for constructing a theoretical model of writing program development" (110). Publishing writing program histories, Barbara L'Eplattenier notes, "is both validation of contemporary scholarship and a logical extension of the contemporary work that has led to the recognition of writing program administration as a scholarly endeavor" (136). At the current moment, however, the historical details necessary for the telling of effective writing program histories are often missing or incomplete: many writing programs (as Rose notes) have no structure for archiving records, and a motive for archiving such materials has been missing because histories of specific programs are not yet recognized in traditional scholarly venues for publication. This book consequently addresses this gap by supplying a close historical examination of a specific writing program and its practices. Further, the book incorporates the kinds of program materials—memos, interviews, textbooks, institutional reports—that Rose identifies as essential to ongoing efforts to document and validate the intellectual work of writing program administration.

To help uncover the conflicting and sometimes ephemeral currents within a particular writing program site, we addressed several key questions, questions that both rely upon and extend the work of previous composition histories:

- How do local cultural, political, and economic conditions affect the ways in which theories of composition are manifested in local classrooms?
- To what degree and to what ends does scholarship in composition influence practices in particular writing programs?
- How do national and international affairs affect writing program development?
- How are curricular designs in composition at specific institutions influenced by the assumptions and beliefs of particular faculty members and administrators?
- How have composition programs in place today developed out of the foundational efforts of critical scholars, administrators, and teachers of the 1970s?

In exploring these questions we focus on a single site and year not because we feel they are the most representative time and topography (though, in retrospect, the year and site now seem to us as representative as anything could be within the diversity of practices known as composition—and seem to offer as well an unusually rich moment and place to reflect upon); nor are we unaware of the limitations of this kind of localized study (our strengths—specificity and depth—are at the expense of breadth). Rather, our concentration on a specific time and topography offers us an opportunity to give an unusually thick, inclusive and instructive description of things in a way that will fill out other histories of the period and that will provide perspective on the present. It also gives us a chance to acknowledge institutional considerations that shape programs and courses, to appreciate the interconnections among instructional efforts like professional writing and composition, and, perhaps most important, to attend to marginal voices and short-lived but instructive developments.

Since we are committed to the complementary propositions that specific circumstances can be explained in part by larger movements and that larger phenomena can be understood through a comprehension of local situations, we have maintained a continuing dialogue between the local and particular, on the one hand, and the broad and general, on the other: we consistently poise an account of developments at Penn State against national and disciplinary developments. Thus, besides offering a perspective on pedagogical practices, past and present, this essay contributes significant, instructive detail to the broad narratives laid out by Berlin, Crowley, Faigley, Harris, Miller, and others even as it offers an additional and telling account of a particular site of composition instruction that is in the tradition of Varnum's study of Amherst College in *Fencing with Words,* Campbell's study of Radcliffe in "Controlling Voices," Hollis's account of the Bryn Mawr Summer School for Women Workers, Simmons's description of Barrett Wendell's pedagogy at Harvard, Gere's study of local sites of literacy formation in *Intimate Practices,* Crowley's analysis of the University of Iowa in *Composition in the University* , and the localized research included in L'Eplattenier and Mastrangelo's *Historical Studies of Writing Program Administration* [5]—historical studies that continue to reflect and identify what writing instruction is as much as what it has been.

2 Background I: The Cultural Scene in 1977

Elvis Presley died on August 16, 1977; in the same month the Hollywood film *Star Wars* was released to record crowds. In retrospect it is easy (probably all too easy) to read the two events as twin signs of the psychic and material stresses that seemed endemic to American life in 1977. Elvis's death denotes for us now yet another endpoint to the 1960s. Elvis and his once-promising era having degenerated together by 1977 into a rather bloated, drug-stupefied, generally aimless, perceptibly aging, terminally ill shell of a decade now come to ruin: the hopeful and revolutionary counter-culture he in some respects represented having been commodified into cynical Las Vegas glitz. Writing in the *Rolling Stone Illustrated History of Rock 'n' Roll* a year before Elvis's death, music critic Peter Graining bemoaned the physical, mental, and moral decline of The King—a decline that seemed to mirror the political and cultural stagnation of the time:

> His hair is dyed, his teeth are capped, his middle is girdled, his voice is a husk, and his eyes film over with glassy impersonality. He [. . .] cannot endure the scorn of strangers, [and] will not go out if his hair isn't right, if his weight—which fluctuates wildly—is not down. He has tantrums onstage and, like some aging politician, is reduced to the ranks of grotesque. (qtd in Rohter and Zito)

Shortly after Elvis's death, *Esquire* painfully juxtaposed the glamour of his public appearance with the physical and psychic degeneration of his person and period: he "occasionally wore dark glasses with ELVIS spelled out on the sides in diamonds [. . . and] owned a gold lamé suit that weighed more than twenty pounds," even though he actually hated the suit, suffered from glaucoma and colitis, and, in recent fits of temper, "was known to smash up television sets and pool tables" (Bradshaw 97). *Star Wars,* meantime, in its characters, setting, and plot nostalgically looked backward to the 1960s. Luke Skywalker, his friends and their adventures provided the wistful cinematic reenactment of a lost children's crusade, flower-powered and anti-establishment (Woodstock Nation This Time Victorious), even as the film offered in Darth Vader the menacing specter of politically conservative forces already poised to sweep out 1960s' liberalism, optimism, prosperity, and interest in social justice. Together the two cultural events testify (if superficially, we know) to how by 1977 the hopes of the previous decade had come mostly to lost promise if not to a sense of outright waste and failure, even to a sense of cultural exhaustion, crisis, and anxiety.

For anxieties there were aplenty in 1977. (For that reason, we should perhaps be using Woody Allen's all-about-anxiety movie *Annie Hall* as the prototypical 1977 cultural artifact, not *Star Wars.*) Political events were still shadowed by the specter of the Watergate era and the crisis in leadership associated with the legacy of Richard Nixon. It is hardly necessary to rehearse how thoroughly Watergate dissipated political power and hope in government in the mid-1970s. That it seems impossible today to recall a single achievement of the Gerald Ford administration—or even to remember anything that *happened* during the Ford administration, except for the pardon of Nixon—speaks to the sense of political ennui that followed Nixon's disgrace, the loss of the war in Vietnam, and the erosion of confidence in 1960s-style national legislation. That Jimmy Carter could defeat Ford in the 1976 election largely on the slogan "I will never lie to the American people" testifies to how demoralized the electorate had become and how character seemed more important than the possibility of social progress through legislative achievement. When he took up the Presidency in 1977, Carter held to a high moral tone, committed himself to human rights initiatives around the world, and achieved a successful peace initiative in the Middle East; but he nevertheless contributed to the crisis in leadership by being unable to act effectively to reverse the nation's serious economic problems and energy shortages. Though unemployment (7.4 percent when Carter took office in January) dropped somewhat during the Carter years, double-digit inflation continued to plague the nation, and the energy predicament seemed so serious and so intractable that in April 1977 the new President created the Department of Energy and declared the situation to be "the moral equivalent of war" and "the greatest challenge our country will face during our lifetime" (418). Carter seemed impotent when he could not get an energy bill through Congress in the summer of 1977 and when, to solve the problem, he urged people to lower thermostats and wear sweaters.

The biggest domestic issues outside the economy and energy seemed to be women's rights and civil rights, but there were setbacks and disappointments in that area too. Over 14,000 women attended the National Women's Conference in Houston in the fall of 1977, but the event was at least as acrimonious as it was invigorating (the abortion issue was particularly divisive); and opposition to the Equal Rights Amendment was now gaining so much support—Phyllis Schlafly was an especially vigorous opponent—that the amendment would ultimately be defeated two years later. In March 1977, an unprecedented number of Americans—probably more than 100,000,000—tuned into the ABC television mini-series *Roots: The Saga of an American Family,* a version of Alex Haley's best-selling (and Pultizer-winning) book of the previous year. But despite the broad appeal of a mini-series devoted to slavery and civil rights, affirmative action programs designed to benefit women and minorities according to Title VII of the Civil Rights Act of 1964 were coming under serious attack. (Indeed, it could be argued that the heroic bootstrap efforts depicted in *Roots* made an implicit and ironic argument against the need for affirmative action.) The most celebrated affront to affirmative action was mounted in the case of Alan Bakke, who sued after his application to medical school at the University of California was rejected in 1974 even as the university had been affirmatively admitting a number of minority students: by 1977, the widely publicized case had reached the Supreme Court.[6] In a not unrelated case, four families living in public housing in Ann Arbor, Michigan, sued the local school district in 1977, charging that lower-class, African American children were not being afforded equal opportunity but were being placed erroneously and disproportionately in special needs classes. The case drew widespread attention, and the racialized meaning of "standard English" came to public consciousness when the plaintiff's attorney drew upon Geneva Smitherman's research on Black English to argue that the language needs of African American children were not being attended to in the schools. And while these controversies were playing out in the news, Anita Bryant, spokeswoman for the Florida orange juice industry, was expressing the views of many by blaming many of the nation's ills on gay citizens and thereby compromising the movement for gay rights. That movement in many ways received its impetus from the famous Stonewall riot in New York City of June 28, 1969, and gay rights parades during the decade frequently commemorated Stonewall as they made their case for civil rights for gays, lesbians, and bisexuals. After 1978, the intensity of those demonstrations intensified because in that year Harvey Milk, an openly gay San Francisco supervisor, was murdered along with the mayor of the city by a notorious bigot, Dan White.

Pennsylvania, the political and economic backdrop of Penn State, offered a microcosm of the nation's political and economic difficulties. State House Speaker Herbert Fineman, in a local reenactment of Watergate, was convicted of obstructing justice for hampering investigations into bribery and the sale of student admissions to professional schools. Governor Milton Shapp, beset by various administrative scandals and rumors that would sweep Republican Richard Thornburgh into office in 1978, fired Commonwealth Secretary C. Dolores Tucker, the highest ranking African-American female state official, on the grounds that she had used her official position as a clearinghouse for personal speaking engagements. This move exacerbated political and racial tensions, as many Pennsylvania residents saw the dismissal of Tucker as racially motivated. Racial and political troubles intensified in Pennsylvania's urban areas as well. In Philadelphia, second-term mayor Frank Rizzo stirred racial tensions by advocating (as early as 1976) the striking of a city charter that prohibited him from serving more than two terms as mayor. The debate around the elimination of the charter was fraught with racial divisiveness. In response to what he interpreted as attempts by black leaders to persuade black voters to reject the proposed city charter amendment, which was to appear on the 1978 ballot, Rizzo asserted that "Whites are going to vote for Rizzo" (qtd. in Featherman and Rosenberg 17). Although Rizzo claimed that his statement was merely an observation about voting habits, his words were widely interpreted as a call for bloc voting by race. In the end the proposed change to the city charter lost by a wide margin, due largely to the resistance of black voters, 96 percent of whom voted against it (2). In 1978 racial tension would express itself again when Philadelphia police, in an attempt to remove members of the African American group MOVE from their communal residence, destroyed whole city blocks in a fire; in the ensuing shootout a police officer was killed and several members of MOVE were injured.

Economically the state epitomized the economic stagnation that in 1977 was plaguing all the states in the nation's industrial "Rustbelt." Despite some good years for agricultural industries and an agreement with Volkswagen to establish a new plant near Pittsburgh in 1976, unemployment in Pennsylvania hovered around the 10 percent mark—or even exceeded it—in many chronically depressed areas (R. Elgin 397). Record-breaking cold in January and February of 1977 depleted natural gas supplies in Pennsylvania, forcing shutdowns at more than 300 plants and temporarily stalling the efforts of over 265,000 workers. In July heavy rains caused a dam to burst near Johnstown, and the subsequent flood killed at least 76 people and caused damage to homes and businesses in excess of $200 million. Confronted with economic problems like these and with diminishing tax revenues consequent upon them, and unable to resolve differences over its budget and necessary tax increases, the state legislature—hopelessly stalemated in the face of the crisis—left the state completely without a budget in 1977. Interstate highways and roads alike were left to rot because the state could not afford repairs. Dead animals piled up on highways and rest areas were closed; citizens began to joke that the state ought to welcome travelers at the borders with the motto "Welcome to Pennsylvania! No Facilities." By August legislators had come up with a partial budget to pay state workers and welfare recipients, but lawmakers continued to debate funding for universities and colleges until early 1978, forcing schools and universities to cut back services and take out temporary loans to meet payrolls. Those loans in turn only compounded budgetary crises for state-funded schools and universities, several of which defaulted because they were unable to make interest payments.

Economic and political problems were only some of the difficulties facing higher education in 1977. Indeed, higher education in general was witnessing extreme instability in the middle 1970s, leading to changes that significantly altered curricula, institutional structures, and student populations. In the fifteen years before 1977, college enrollments had burgeoned, particularly among previously underrepresented groups. Pennsylvania alone witnessed a 21 percent increase in enrollments in higher education during the 1970s, with the greatest growth coming between 1973 and 1976. Widely discussed "open admissions policies" (started in 1970 at the City College of New York

[CUNY]) along with federal, state, and local affirmative action policies put the highly charged issue of accommodating culturally diverse students at the center of debates in higher education.[7] Enrollment for African Americans in higher education increased from 821,930 in 1974 to 960,804 in 1978; similar increases were recorded for Hispanics (287,432 to 370,366), Asians (114,266 to 203,250), and Native Americans (52,876 to 66,264)—numbers that would continue to increase through the 1980s (Deskins 20). Furthermore, federal measures such as Title IX (1972) were continuing to ease access for female students. For instance, although men still outnumbered women 61 percent to 39 percent in the student body at large, a majority of the 1977 freshman class at Penn State was female. Older students, or "returning adult students," were also swelling the ranks: by 1976, learners over the age of 22 were the fastest growing segment in higher education, constituting 48 percent of the total national enrollment of 10 million (Munday 681). At the same time, administrators debated both the legality and the practicality of governmental measures to increase the numbers of previously underrepresented groups on campus. When places like Columbia, Cornell, Harvard, and Michigan faced threats from the federal government to withhold funding if they did not move more resolutely to increase enrollment of underrepresented groups, many in higher education lashed out against such "federal intrusion" (Brubacher and Rudy 79)[8]; but mostly universities moved to comply.

Demands for more accessible and professionally applicable higher education led to another trend in higher education in the 1970s: the increasing influence of community colleges, two-year junior colleges, and professional/technical schools, all of which brought higher education closer to increasing numbers of students. In a 1976 report, for example, the Pennsylvania Department of Education claimed that "both the number of community colleges and the increasing number of students at such colleges have constituted the greatest growth in post-secondary education in Pennsylvania" (i). Students at the community colleges either worked for associate degrees or transferred after two years to complete baccalaureate requirements: Temple University in Philadelphia was receiving over a thousand transfers a year in 1977, many from Philadelphia Community College (Pennsylvania Dept. of Education 6); and the Penn State system had grown to include 18 two-year campuses, many of whose students came to University Park from those Commonwealth Campuses to complete traditional undergraduate degrees.[9] Proprietary schools and schools of technology grew even faster than community colleges during the 1970s. In Pennsylvania, for example, enrollment in proprietary and technical schools grew an astounding 184 percent from 1970 to 1979 (Pennsylvania Economy League 3).

Despite these increases in overall enrollment in the first half of the 1970s, many colleges and universities faced great economic challenges as they confronted inflation, rising energy costs, and a projected dearth in the number of college-age students (indeed, that anticipated dearth explains, as much as do the political forces left over from the 1960s, the willingness of colleges to reach out to under-represented groups and returning-adult students). Even as early as 1971, a survey of 41 institutions conducted by the Carnegie Commission found that 71 percent were either already in financial distress or were well on their way to it (Brubacher and Rudy 383). In Pennsylvania, for example, federal appropriations to higher education grew nearly 106 percent during the decade while state and local appropriations increased over 92 percent (Pennsylvania Economy League 3), but those increases could not keep pace with rising expenses. Costs for instruction rose nearly 110 percent, expenditures for operation and maintenance of university grounds and buildings climbed nearly 135 percent, and a Pennsylvania government struggling with hard economic times was reluctant to spend additional money on higher education. According to the Pennsylvania State Board of Education, the state ranked 20th—well above average—among the states in its per capita income, underutilized tax capacity, and level of employment but only 48th in terms of higher education appropriations as a percentage of state general revenue (45).

Many universities therefore were reducing faculty and staff; articles in higher education journals were regularly offering administrators advice on "Managing Faculty Reductions" (e.g., Alm, Erhle, and Webster 153). A study of 163 institutions conducted in 1975 found that from 1971–1974, 74 percent of private four-year institutions, 66 percent of public four-year institutions, and 41 percent of two-year institutions had undergone staff reductions (Alm, Erhle, and Webster 153). In 1973–74, the University of Wisconsin sent lay-off notices to 88 of its tenured faculty; Southern Illinois dismissed 104 faculty and staff members, 28 of them tenured (Brubacher and Rudy 384); and Michigan's public universities, in the face of setbacks in the auto industry that reduced tax revenues sharply, were under similar duress. Several institutions even faced the possibility of closing. In response to these pressing economic conditions, faculty and staff stepped up efforts to protect their jobs by unionizing. By June 1974, faculty had selected collective bargaining agents on 338 campuses and had successfully unionized on 29 (Brubacher and Rudy 392). Colleges and universities sought to manage budget problems not only by reducing their faculties but also by increasing part-time positions and graduate assistantships. According to the National Center for Educational Statistics, the five-year period from 1972 to 1977 saw a dramatic increase in the number of part-time faculty in higher education: in 1972, colleges and universities employed 3.17 fulltimers for every part-time faculty member; in 1977, the numbers had fallen to 1.26 fulltimers for every parttimer (Leslie, Kellams, and Gunne 23).

The panic over declining funds was exacerbated by frequent predictions of large enrollment drops—the general consensus was at least 15 percent—for the coming decade. According to the projections of the Pennsylvania Economy League, for instance, enrollments in higher education in Pennsylvania would drop 32.1 percent during the 1980s, with state-related institutions like Penn State losing close to 20 percent of their enrollment numbers (2–3). Another report issued by the Pennsylvania State Board of Education in 1978 suggested that, due to changes in the birth rate after 1960, "the number of college-aged youths 18–22 w[ould] drop by about 24 percent between 1975 and 1990" (43).

Economic conditions and projected declines in enrollment caused many potential students to reconsider the value of higher education. On the one hand, this convergence of crises resulted in a phenomenon known as "student consumerism." To keep the customers coming, institutions of higher education had to please those customers. *The Educational Record* dedicated a series of articles in the Spring 1977 issue to "The Student Consumer Movement." As their titles reveal, these articles explained how to maintain "Consumer Interest in Higher Education" (Hoy 180) and provided examples of how some institutions had been "Meeting Student Demands" (Moye 191). The *Record* also included a study of student views of good teaching, again reflecting the desire to please the students, who, the writers of the article claimed, "are the consumers of instruction" (Morstain and Gaff 300). Teacher training and "retraining" gained in popularity, again in response to the perceived changes brought about in the university by changing student populations and declining budgets, and "faculty development" became an academic buzzword. Jerry G. Gaff, Director of the Project for Institutional Renewal, boasted that, as of 1977, "a recent national survey estimated that approximately 50 percent of all institutions of higher education have a program or set of practices identified as faculty development" (Morstain and Gaff 299). Jon Wergin, Elizabeth Mason and Paul Munson, all involved at the time in educational planning and development at the Medical College of Virginia, directly linked faculty development emphases to the increasing call for public accountability and to the impact of student consumerism: "Faculty development is fast emerging as a priority in post-secondary education. Reasons for this surge of interest are numerous, but most center around traditionally nonacademic concerns. Demands from students and society are becoming increasingly strident for educational programs that are accountable to their needs" (289).

On the other hand, universities contemplated curricular changes in response to the economic situation and changed climate on campus. Humanities departments and colleges of liberal arts in particular faced immense challenges. With an unprecedented number of new students entering the academy, with the growing popularity of technical education, and with enrollments booming in community colleges and other two-year institutions, many in higher education worried about a decline in students' appreciation of the value of a liberal arts education. In the *Educational Record* for Winter 1977, Edward Eddy (soon to become Provost at Penn State) forecasted a substantial decline in the fortunes of liberal arts education. According to Eddy, students in the 1970s were "less skilled and yet more pragmatic than their predecessors" (9). Students used to be concerned with "being better," he lamented, but now they were just concerned with "being better off." Eddy wasn't alone in his beliefs. In a 1976 book, Geoffrey Wagner, a professor of English who taught basic writing at City College of New York (CUNY), called open admissions "The End of Education." One reviewer scored the vehemence of such arguments against expanding higher education by explaining Wagner's book as "a politically and educationally conservative polemic" (529) that promoted the university as "a place where knowledge is pursued objectively for its own sake, an institution concerned with higher things, free of mundane pressures" (Lane 529).

Similar concerns were evident in controversies over increasing disciplinary specialization. An editorial in the *Educational Record* for

Winter 1977 attacked the "divisiveness" of academic specialization and called for an end of "fractionization" that was harming the holistic benefits of a "total system" of liberal arts education (Heyns 4). Summing up the panic over the place of liberal arts in 1970s higher education, Stephen Bailey, Vice President of the American Council on Education, lamented, "How can liberal learning accommodate the twin necessities of educating specialists and educating generalists, of turning out experts who are not merely technicians?" (250). In the struggle to accommodate the new students brought in by expanding admissions and to respond to growing public concern about the ultimate goals of higher education, the 1970s generated much curricular reform. Attempts to establish core curricula and programs in "basic skills" which might equalize and unite the increasingly diverse student population grew in popularity. Bailey, for example, advocated a "liberal core" of courses and attention to "basic skills" (which, for him, meant "spelling and grammar" [251]). Support for such centralized "essential" curricula received a boost when Harvard shifted from general education requirements to a core curriculum, even though that curriculum promised to exclude many of the "new students." In the February 7, 1977 issue of *The Chronicle of Higher Education,* the team of curriculum evaluators from Harvard defended their move to a core curriculum by identifying six "basic" characteristics of the educated person, including "the ability to think and write clearly"; "an awareness of other cultures"; "good manners and high aesthetic and moral standards"; and "depth in some field of knowledge" (10). The ideal student, then, would be both a specialist and a generalist—and maintain the manners and aesthetic values associated with the Ivy elite.

From faculty pens and mouths across the country came nostalgic laments about the "State of the Humanities" (Reager 148). In the February 1977 *Harper's,* English professor Reed Whittemore sounded a gloomy death knell for the humanities, which he predicted would all too soon "go the way of the classics" (qtd. in Gregg 13). Penn State liberal arts faculty, in the spirit of the national mood, clearly felt these pressures and responded in the spring of 1977 by convening a faculty conference at University Park to ponder the future of "The College of Liberal Arts in the 1980's." The published proceedings of the conference, which involved over 600 faculty from 20 campuses, reflected the concerns plaguing humanities scholars across the nation. Penn State Liberal Arts faculty concerns were heightened by 1977 figures that showed a 32 percent relative decline in College of Liberal Arts enrollments over the course of the 1970s (Coelen 40). Liberal Arts Dean Stanley Paulson's "Introduction" to the published proceedings set the tone for the papers and discussions to follow and clearly linked the concerns fronted at the conference to larger issues in higher education:

> The readers of this volume will no doubt be struck with the way questions and problems outnumber the answers and solutions. For it to have been otherwise would have been to evade or oversimplify the complex changes underway in the larger society as well as in a university of 50,000 students. [. . .] Though the Conference participants looked unblinkingly at the problems liberal education now confronts, the ability of the liberal arts to deal with the developing educational needs was affirmed again and again. While they recognized the current pressures toward vocationalism and technological specialization, the long range importance of preparation for life rather than simply to make a living was stressed. (2)

Mirroring the concerns expressed by Provost-elect Eddy and the Vice President of the American Council on Education, Stephen Bailey, Paulson stressed the conference's importance in maintaining the unity of the liberal arts in the face of increasing demands for job-related education. Bailey, in fact, delivered the keynote of the Penn State Conference. Defending the need for liberal education, Bailey described the tenuous human condition to the conference participants in a way that speaks to the unhappy temper of the time and situation:

> Perched on a whirling planet, blind to our origins, blind to our reasons for being, we wander between a desolate sense that we are bits of transient nothingness, and a strange sense of presence of ineffable innuendoes that mock our despair. Whatever the long-range fate of the universe, we have a continuing commitment in education to discover and transmit truths that are in fact fertile hypotheses about the reality, and the latent possibilities, of the existence we know and of the existence we can anticipate for our children. (11)

3 Background II: English Studies in 1977

Given the sense of crisis and malaise in the university and in the humanities, it is not surprising that a similar atmosphere was evident in English studies. The discipline was still perceived to be a key component of all university training, yet the field was nevertheless experiencing economic and intellectual challenges that prompted heated debate.

Most obviously, English was experiencing a severe budgetary crunch at a time when the humanities (like every other discipline) were being more and more gauged in quantitative terms. Enrollments in English in the 1970s plummeted almost everywhere. Nationally the number of English undergraduate degrees awarded plunged from an all time high of 63,976 in academic year 1971–1972 to 35,328 in 1977–78—the lowest figure in many years (National Center, tables 229 and 230). Of all bachelors' degrees granted in 1978, fewer than four percent were now in English (Neel and Nelson 51–53) as compared to 7.59 percent in 1968 (Franklin 6). In most cases the drop-off from the heady days of the 1960s was unexpected and calamitous as English faculty without much preparation or data or prior experience debated what to do in the face of alarmingly diminishing enrollments in introductory and upper-division courses.

At the same time, despite the sharp decline in English undergraduate degrees granted during the late 1970s, English graduate programs resolutely continued to confer an increasing number of PhDs for a job market that had recently and precipitously collapsed. During the 1960s, the number of English graduate programs had increased over 50 percent, from 81 to 124 (Geckle 43), and new PhD programs continued to appear on campuses during the 1970s. At the same time, job opportunities were suddenly decreasing so that by 1977 a significant glut of doctorate holders existed in relation to the number of vacant tenure-track positions in English. Appointments in literary studies decreased by over 65 percent between 1972 and 1978; in the class of 1978, 40 percent of all English doctorates were unable to obtain any appointment, and another 20 percent were forced to accept temporary, often part-time, teaching jobs (Neel and Nelson 51–53).[10] *Time* magazine, describing the 1977 MLA convention in its January 9, 1978 issue, noted that "Of the 1094 PhDs created last year in English and 753 in foreign languages, we learn that only 42 percent and 46 percent respectively have landed steady teaching positions" of any kind. And the future seemed just as bleak: Ernest R. May, chair of the history department at Harvard, estimated that "whereas now [1977] the humanities can expect 16,000 new jobs annually, by the 1980s there will be only 4,000 (600–700 of those in English)" (qtd. in Geckle 43). Jasper Neel, then director of MLA's English programs, and Jeanne C. Nelson wrote that "there is absolutely no reason to believe that more than 35 percent of recent doctorates will be able to make a lifelong career of college English teaching. [. . .] There won't be an upturn in PhD hiring in this century" (51).

Reluctantly recognizing the end of the baby boom and the resulting decrease in students, the MLA and other academic organizations arranged conferences to encourage and foster professional employment

Sidebar: The Birth of TOPOI

Hugh Burns

In just 1977, when the world was more analog than digital, before word processors had replaced typewriters, when consultants were paid big bucks to explain the differences between hardware and software, I started programming computers.

Two years before, the United States Congress had created a line item in the personnel budget of the United States Air Force Academy mandating that the Department of Defense authorize one "slot" for a certified doctoral rhetorician to direct composition and speech courses in Colorado Springs so that future Air Force generals would not receive poorly reasoned, poorly edited,

for English professionals outside of academia (one at Emory University in 1978; another at the University of Maryland in 1979), but the sense of crisis in the job market continued as the media publicized the disappearance of college teaching opportunities in English and related disciplines. By the late 1970s, the growth spurt in graduate English studies of the 1960s had therefore evaporated. After a 6.5 percent increase in graduate students between 1974 and 1975, a notable decline in graduate student applications soon followed, and many departments were hard pressed to fill assistantships with capable applicants. Dual-degree programs, combining English with a second major such as Business Administration or Library Science, became a functional solution that many universities tried (Geckle), while others (as the MLA convention program for 1977 indicates) welcomed computer instruction, technical writing, and curricular revisions that spoke implicitly of the momentum toward a more consumer-based atmosphere on university campuses.[11]

Two subfields bucked the trend in decreasing enrollments. One was creative writing, which maintained steady enrollments and faculty appointments at many colleges and universities. But despite strong interest in their courses, creative writers were nevertheless struggling intellectually over the relative merits of alternative pedagogies. The Associated Writing Programs (the creative writing equivalent of the

and massively stupid letters from second lieutenants—or so I was told.

In any event I was ordered to conclude my duties as a detachment Commander outfitted in fatigues on the eleven-square mile island of Ie Shima in the middle of the East China Sea and to PCS (permanently change station) to the University of Texas at Austin to complete a PhD in rhetoric—before returning to the USAF Academy as Course Director of Composition and Speech. In January 1977, I arrived on the spacious forty acres at the University of Texas at Austin and began my doctoral program.

On a Monday in January, I attended my first rhetoric course—and my first computer science course. By day and in a well-window-lit seminar room, I was led by James L. Kinneavy through Aristotle's *Rhetoric,* chapter by chapter, proof by proof, enthymeme by enthymeme, counterpart by counterpart, to recover the wonders of heuristics and the available designs of verbal reasoning

MLA or CCCC) categorized the nation's creative writing programs in their annual catalogue based on each institution's emphasis on writing. The three categories as defined by AWP were Studio (featuring a central focus on student writing practice), Studio/Academic (emphasizing equally both writing and literature), and Traditional Literary Study and Creative Writing (offering central focus on mastery of literature). Though a preference was not explicitly stated in the catalogue, the AWP's discussions of the three different types leaned in the direction of the studio method (*AWP Catalogue* 1–6). Throughout the decade, within creative writing the reading component lost ground to writing, based on the craft-centered workshop model made famous by the University of Iowa. According to that model, the "writer" (as an unproblematized, unitary, relatively autonomous consciousness) and the products of that writer remained at the center of the curriculum and the classroom. The utility of literature courses in the education of creative writers was debated throughout the decade.

The other growth area in English studies, of course, was composition and related enterprises like technical writing and business writing. Virtually all English departments experienced growth in composition courses during the 1970s, usually substantial growth. But as numbers increased in composition courses, public outcry over student writing deficiencies also forcibly tested the validity of prevailing approaches

about uncertainty. By night and in an underground computing center, I was guided by George H. Culp loop-by-loop, string-by-string, and if-then-by-goto-statement, to discover the delights of algorithms and the available designs of mathematical reasoning about certainty. For weeks, sealed up in the basement of UT's Parlin Hall between book cases and working with two dumb terminals hardwired (thanks to Susan Wittig's National Science Foundation Grant) to a Digital DEC-10 mainframe computer in the Humanities Research Center off Guadalupe drag, I wrote computer programs that "knew" the answers to every clever multiple-choice or true-false question I could think to ask about English grammar and American literature. I programmed software to respond either "Correct" or "Incorrect" to such questions as "True or false? The principal principle for principals principally is to be principled." Then, just as the blue bonnets started painting the

to composition instruction. Students, on the whole and on the average, *were* less skilled in 1977 than their predecessors, according to the available measurement tools. Scholastic Aptitude Test (SAT) scores for incoming freshmen continued along a fifteen-year slide as more and more high school graduates took the tests in preparation for college admission. Between 1977 and 1978 alone, average scores on the SAT at Penn State dropped 21 points. Over 25 percent of incoming freshmen at Penn State now tested as deficient in basic English skills and required remedial English instruction (Unsigned article). Meanwhile, the new open admissions policies of junior and community colleges were perpetuating the need for remedial composition. When CUNY began open admissions in New York, questions arose throughout academia concerning the very role of a university education in American culture, and remediation—especially in the area of composition—swiftly became a national priority for universities struggling to maintain their enrollment numbers. As the population of what would be considered traditional college students declined in general, student enrollment figures were maintained through a new student population—one that was believed to be in need of remedial help.

The call for remediation coincided with, if not outright triggered, the perceived need to emphasize and overhaul the teaching of English composition on most university campuses. *Newsweek*'s publication of

Texas hill country, I had an idea: what if computers were stupid and humans were smart, what would happen?

In other words, what if the principal principles of designing computer-assisted instruction were not certain? What would happen if, following Aristotle's first enthymeme topic in his *Rhetoric* about considering opposites, I started programming computers not to "know" the correct answer it transmitted to the green CRT screen? Would users suspend disbelief? Would my punch cards be bent, mutilated, or torn? Would my graduate committee allow me to bring an analytical engine into Parlin Hall's humanities garden? Would I have any friends outside of this basement? Would I graduate? Would I eventually prevent second lieutenants from sending poorly reasoned, poorly edited, and massively stupid letters to three-star generals? Would, more importantly, writers invent better arguments, find better evidence, and truly search for the available means of persuasion?

the cover story "Why Johnny Can't Write" in December of 1975 hammered home the case for sweeping reform and for a "back-to-basics" approach to writing instruction. In assaults from the public media, just about everyone was to blame—television, parents, teachers, universities, and methods of testing. Academic discourse on the issue surfaced in professional journals, university publications, and faculty bulletins; fluency versus correctness, speech idioms versus written idioms, and the value of literature versus rhetorical constructs were among the most prevalent topics of debate. Whatever the cause of the perceived decline in writing ability (and in retrospect it seems apparent that the "decline" was really a manifestation of the expansion of the student body), students, employers, deans, and the media had grown alarmed and moved to correct what they thought was wrong with composition. Out of that weighty tasking, the discipline of rhetoric and composition became professionalized as never before. Reaction in the field to "Why Johnny Can't Write" solidified the existing sense of urgency and became the principle justification for reform. The prevailing responses to the article identified a need to promote literacy by increasing attentiveness to remediation, process, and individualized curricula.[12]

While composition was becoming the center of public and professional controversy, English as a discipline also seemed to be in crisis and transition. Although traditional literary scholarship retained

And so it happened. In 1977, I wrote a computer program called TOPOI. The program invited writers to answer open-ended questions derived from Aristotle's twenty-eight enthymemes on topics of their choice. I programmed in BASIC and the computer did what I asked it to do: stimulate one writer at a time to discover, recover, wonder, or think about their definitions and key terms; their reasons to trust, their explanations, and their specific details; their private opinions, their public perceptions, their causes and effects; their costs, conditions, and better ways; their responsibilities to research in libraries, archives, and even books. There was no time limit. There was no final score. There was no right answer. There was only a close encounter of the rhetorical invention kind. There were only questions. A dissertation followed.

In 1977, I first asked not what my students could do for me on a dumb terminal, but what I could do for my students with all the available means of technology. In 1977, I learned that I could

much of its prestige in the field—close readings of canonical works remained a staple of *PMLA* and other flagship journals, and E. D. Hirsch's brilliant books on critical theory maintained many traditional theoretical assumptions—it was nevertheless becoming clear that the New Criticism was showing serious signs of age and incompetence, and that the days were numbered when a stable canon of literary works could continue to provide the basis for English studies. The problem was that no one knew quite what to do instead of New Criticism and the study of canonical works. Semiotic, structuralist, phenomenological, and psychoanalytic approaches to literary texts were prominent in the late 1960s and into the 1970s (Umberto Eco's *A Theory of Semiotics* appeared in 1976, for instance), but most scholars nevertheless remained unengaged and even confused by these critical schools. Beginning in the mid-1970s there was a move away from structuralism toward deconstruction, on the one hand, and more social forms of criticism, on the other. While Jacques Derrida had appeared at the Johns Hopkins conference on structuralism as early as 1966, his works remained untranslated and rather obscure until 1973, when *Speech and Phenomena* appeared in English and deconstruction began to emerge as a major subject for debate. Derrida's *Of Grammatology* was translated in 1976, and Paul de Man's essays (many of them collected in his 1979 book *Allegories of Reading*) began to domesticate Derridean thought. Other Continental theorists were simultaneously taking scholarship away from textual dynamics and toward a consideration of readers and their social contexts. Roland Barthes proclaimed "the death of the author" in his 1977 *Image—Music—Text;* Hans Robert Jauss and Wolfgang Iser were contributing reception theory and

program a computer to be artificially intelligent, and I was proud of it. In 1977, with a deeper sense of purpose and audience, I began to teach by asking students what they thought about, what they wanted to say, what they wanted write about, and what they wanted to do for others.

True or false? A principal pioneering computational rhetorician is still asking questions and still investigating human creativity, humane consciousness, and harmonious chaos.

❦

reader-response to the American theory wars; and Stanley Fish, Norman Holland, David Bleich, and others (many of them collected in Jane Tompkins's 1980 book, *Reader-Response Criticism*) picked up on audience-centered criticism and developed it in novel, stimulating, and controversial ways. Fredric Jameson's neo-Marxist criticism (e.g., *Marxism and Form,* 1971) gained adherents and allies, among them Frank Lentricchia, Edward Said, and Gayatri Spivak; J. A. Austin's *How to Do Things with Words,* the seminal text on speech-act theory, appeared in 1975; and Michel Foucault's English publication of *Discipline and Punish* (1977) and *Power/Knowledge: Selected Interviews and other Writings, 1972–1977* was beginning to refocus attention on the conditions of textual production within culture. Similarly, feminists such as Judith Fetterley (*The Resisting Reader*, 1978), Elaine Showalter (*A Literature of Their Own*, 1977), Nina Baym (*Women's Fiction*, 1978), and others were redirecting attention to women writers, talking about reading from a gendered position, and in other ways inventing a critical position that would prosper in spite of controversy for years. During the 1970s, literally hundreds of colleges and universities began women's studies programs. As women writers entered the canon or coexisted alongside it, the canon itself became undermined as a stable given of English departments. Thus, new writers and kinds of writing entered the discipline as objects of study and the essays of theorists themselves seemed to be making a strong, if ironic, bid for canonicity, challenging distinctions between "primary" and "secondary" texts, and "literature" and "theory." Was theory offering new frameworks for the study of literature and language, or was it just another subdiscipline? Were English professors now expected to neglect literary texts in favor of theory? Was it necessary, in the light of new theoretical approaches and canon revision, to redesign the English curriculum?

In one sense, of course, all of this intellectual activity was invigorating, and the rebirth of English studies that is evident in the healthy discipline of today might be understood as beginning with the ferment of the 1970s. Wayne Booth's plea for tolerance and pluralism in his 1979 *Critical Understanding: The Power and Limits of Pluralism* demonstrated that new developments were not necessarily the sign that the barbarians were at the gates. But at the time, the turmoil did paralyze a great many teachers of English, many of whom seemed at odds with one another. "As a profession we are today so diversified in our interests—one might say fragmented—that we do not seem to have much to say to our collective self," wrote the editor of *PMLA,* William Schaefer, as he concluded his term at the beginning of 1978. As we will see, this sense of intellectual ferment also influenced the conduct of composition in 1977.

We don't mean to paint an entirely negative portrait of the state of the Union, higher education, and English studies in 1977. There were exhilarating moments and positive developments too in the wake of the celebration of the nation's bicentennial in 1976. Achievements in the space program thrilled Americans, and Rocky Balboa triumphed over Apollo Creed (as Alex Haley's ancestors had triumphed over tremendous adversity in *Roots*) in a manner that somehow vindicated American individualism and ethnicities. Not for nothing was Debby Boone's "You Light Up My Life" the sunny and bright Song of the Year 1977. But from our current perspective it is difficult to understand the 1970s in general and 1977 in particular as anything less than anxious and difficult.

4 Composition in 1977: The National Conversation

What might be done in response to all of these difficulties, all of this sense of crisis and controversy, all of this attention to the nation's literacy woes? That was the problem that faced writing teachers and professionals struggling to develop the field of rhetoric and composition in 1977. There was no shortage of solutions proposed by departments of English that were using composition as a place to work out their own difficulties and that were in the midst of being both challenged and galvanized intellectually.

Old Time Religions: Traditionalism and Current Traditionalism

Not every proposed solution was innovative, of course. As you might expect from the counter-reformation voices we quoted in the previous chapter, some people prescribed a stiff dose of traditional medicines: a focus on the expository modes and/or on " basic skills," a Great Books curriculum, and other measures associated with what Richard Young in an essay published in 1978 dubbed "current-traditionalism" in composition.[13] Young's essay called attention to the resiliency of current-traditional pedagogy in the nation's composition courses: the "emphasis on the composed product rather than the composing process; an analysis of discourse into description, narration, exposition, and argument; the strong concern with usage (syntax, spelling, punctuation) and style (economy, clarity, emphasis); the preoccupation with the informal essay and research paper" (31). Proceeding from a positivist, "windowpane" view toward language, current traditionalism depended on the publication of handbooks to reinforce its obsession with correctness and with static forms such as the five-paragraph essay and the research paper. To teachers of writing who lacked formal training and who were comfortable teaching as they had been taught themselves, current traditionalism offered a formulaic approach to invention (if invention was considered at all), a linear view of composing that reduced revision pretty much to correction, and a "bottom-up," not a "top down," approach to instruction (i.e., instruction began with words, sentences, and then paragraphs, rather than proceeding from overall plans and strategies that then generate local sentences and paragraphs). Many teachers of current-traditionalism, dedicated and experienced or not, mainly understood themselves to be assignors and correctors of papers that tended to be required year after year; learning to compose was regarded largely as a matter of learning rules for logic and etiquette.[14]

For many teachers of writing, learning to write was also a matter of learning forms known as the expository modes. Advocates of the so-called modes—description, narration, exposition, and argumentation—could trace their instruction to the nineteenth-century work of Alexander Bain, who held that each mode had "its own subject matter, its own organizational forms, and its own language" (D'Angelo, *Conceptual* 115); descriptive writing organizes, narrative writing recounts, expository writing instructs, argumentative writing persuades. Although Robert Connors has claimed that Bain's modal curriculum effectively died by the 1950s as exposition came to dominate the other modes ("Rise and Fall"), in fact it appears more accurate to us to say that the modes were simply being renegotiated—their number, their functions, their relationships. Any number of textbooks and readers and courses were still organized according to some version of the modes, and in those courses students were directed through a series of modal assignments, one after the next, that were illustrated in the readers. A description assignment might be followed by narration, comparison, analysis, classification, and definition—or some other combination might be offered. In other words, if exposition was gaining headway as the chief kind of mode, it was also generating its own kind of modal arrangements: static forms of one kind or another into which, according to current-traditional thinking, students were implored to pour information.

These current-traditional approaches to writing instruction were welcomed into many English departments in part because of the long history of New Criticism in those departments. After a text-based pedagogy for criticism was created by the publication of Cleanth Brooks and Robert Penn Warren's *Understanding Poetry* in 1938, John Crowe Ransom's *The New Criticism* in 1941, and Rene Wellek and Austin Warren's *Theory of Literature* in 1942, many writing courses began to incorporate New Critical values. New Critical faith in the autonomy of art and artists, and New Critical respect for stylistic achievement, easily dovetailed with current traditionalism, which also eschewed politics and emphasized style; and New Critical regard for written artifacts over artistic processes or cultural and rhetorical contexts reinforced current-traditional pedagogical doctrine as well. New Critics walled off so-called "literary" (and hence "timeless") discourses from everyday ones, insisting on distinguishing the special connotative beauty of literary language from matter-of-fact scientific denotation. New Critics quite literally gave rhetoric a bad name, regarding everyday discourses as beneath their consideration, and their disdain for what they regarded as ephemeral writing translated itself in many composition classes into attention to Great Works and Great Writers, as opposed to student writing and more popular and rhetorical culture. It is true that by 1977 the New Criticism was losing momentum, as we have indicated: close analyses of literary texts had become stale with every new microanalysis, and even Rene Wellek was seeing its shortcomings in the famous essay he was writing in 1977, "The New Criticism: Pros and Cons." But New Criticism and current traditionalism continued to affect classroom practices well into the next decade—even as they affect classrooms today.

Indeed, at many colleges and universities during the 1970s the composition class comfortably doubled as an introduction to Great Ideas or to canonical literary texts that were part of an established literary canon that provided "content" for students to write about. A number of composition-and-literature textbooks accommodated these courses, as they had for decades (Crowley, *Composition,* chapter 5). If the courses did not always emphasize explicitly literary genres of poetry, drama, and fiction, then they often offered up an analogous "canon" of "artistic" nonfiction or an introduction to Great Ideas in the sciences, the arts, and the humanities that could generate material for student essays. The best-selling 1977 edition of *The Norton Reader,* for example, accommodated both approaches: it included familiar essays by people like E.B. White, Wallace Stegner, Virginia Woolf, Thomas Jefferson, James Thurber, Niccolo Machiavelli, Jacob Bronowski, Loren Eiseley, John Henry Newman, X. J. Kennedy, Ralph Waldo Emerson, Jonathan Swift, and George Orwell ("A Modest Proposal" and "Politics and the English Language" to be sure), along with 1960s-inspired items by Eldridge Cleaver, Dee Brown, George Jackson, Martin Luther King, Jr., and Toni Morrison; and it organized itself according to heady titles like History, Ethics, Human Nature, Education, Mind, Politics and Government, and Literature and the Arts. (For that matter, it offered a table of contents that permitted teachers to teach the expository modes from the book as well.) Current traditionalism in 1977 was fed by many other textbooks in the Norton tradition and many other handbooks in the Harbrace tradition: enthusiastic imitation followed imitation.

Process Pedagogies

But criticism of New Critical and current-traditional approaches to composition was coming from several sources, among them the proponents of two student-centered pedagogies with roots in the 1960s and in the social sciences: expressivism and cognitivism. Besides being mutually convinced of the relative autonomy of writers from social circumstances (still something of a given in the 1970s), both expressivists and cognitivists claimed to be fundamentally concerned with the "composing process" of writers: they therefore promoted what we now know as "process pedagogies." But the two groups treated the composing process somewhat differently and expected different behaviors from student writers. Though there was actually considerable common ground between the two camps, in 1977 expressivist and cognitivist advocates of process were in fact competing for priority in the field and promoting different basic principles and pedagogical strategies.[15]

Expressivists, who during the 1960s had ridiculed traditional composition classrooms for promoting humdrum current-traditional formulas and a neutral voice that Ken Macrorie had dubbed "Engfish," accommodated process pedagogies in the 1970s rather easily. Indeed, when back-to-basics advocates attacked personal voice pedagogies and the creativity-oriented classroom tactics of the expressivists, expressivists often defended themselves by adopting a process perspective. In his 1972 book *The Authentic Voice: A Pre-Writing Approach to Student Writing,* for example, Donald Stewart (following Robert Zoellner, and Gordon Rohman and Albert Wlecke) had blamed contemporary teachers for using methods that "teach students how to *judge* their finished work but not how to produce it"—a development which, Stewart went on to say, "implies a fundamental shift in attention away from the *product* of writing toward the *process* by which that product eventually gets on paper" (19). Along with Macrorie, William Coles, Donald Murray, and Peter Elbow, Stewart argued that student writing would improve if students could be given the opportunity and the space to exercise their writing abilities extensively, especially in the earliest stages of the writing process. Accordingly, what were known as "pre-writing techniques" and other process-oriented strategies (e.g., free writing, reflective writing, journal keeping), essential expressivist pedagogies designed to promote student growth through writing, were promoted for the composition classroom to achieve the expressivist aims of personal growth, authenticity, self-discovery, and voice:

> The primary goal of any writing course is self-discovery for the student and [. . .] the most visible indication of that self-discovery is the appearance, in the student's writing, of an authentic voice. It proceeds from the second conviction that the techniques of pre-writing, developed in the 1960s, will best help the student develop this authentic voice. (Stewart, Preface xii)

While expressivists agreed about the importance of the writing process, they committed themselves to somewhat different specific approaches. Coles, an iconoclastic product of Theodore Baird's writer-centered pedagogies at Amherst (see Varnum) who had become the composition director at Pittsburgh (where he influenced David Bartholomae, who arrived about the same time), was teaching students to develop an effective, individual style that would emerge if they would write frequently about their personal viewpoints and experiences, discuss their writing with others, and use the responses of others (rather than formal rules) to guide their revisions. In *The Plural I* (1978), Coles in the vein of Macrorie denounced "themewriting" as the inevitable result of most current composition pedagogy and encouraged students to become adept at more expressive than formulaic communications. Elbow in a similar vein was contending that people learn to write not from textbooks but from actually writing and reflecting on that writing; his *Writing without Teachers* (1973) provided prompts that encouraged a variety of activities, from freewriting to reflection to exchange. While he was careful to emphasize that his approach was designed ultimately to produce better written products, Elbow was widely appreciated for encouraging writers to explore freely their developing thoughts through multiple drafts. And he was adamant about the need to deflect critical attention away from formal matters, including correctness, until very late in the composing process. But Elbow's approach was not asocial: while he emphasized the need for students to develop personal identities through writing, he also encouraged them to consider audiences for their documents and to learn how to function in communities through discourse. In an appendix to *Writing without Teachers,* Elbow offered "The Doubting Game and the Believing Game" as a dialectical process of measuring the claims of the self against those of the community.

As the title *Writing without Teachers* implies, expressivists fundamentally held that formal instruction was more or less incidental to a writer's growth. Students were regarded as independent agents—even teachers and textbooks were irrelevant—who could intuit principles of effective writing through trial and error. The material of writing came from the student's own subjective background, the teacher could "never quarrel with the student's experience" (Elbow 106), and a writing course was thus a matter of a teacher's nurturing student self-discovery and self-expression. All of these values were already guiding the pedagogy of Donald Murray, who would nurture expressivism into the 1980s: in 1977 Murray was developing an expressivist-process synthesis that was beholden to creative writing workshops and that would find its most mature expression first in his 1978 publication "Write Before Writing" and then in his 1980 "Writing As Process: How Writing Finds Its Own Meaning." All of these values were also getting theoretical sanction from the instructive sections on expressive discourse in James Kinneavy's *A Theory of Discourse* (1971) and from James Britton's appreciation of expressive discourse in *Language and Learning* (1970) and *The Development of Writing Abilities* (1975; the American paperback edition appeared first in 1977).

In their concern for self-discovery rather than communicative effectiveness, however, expressivists clashed with those in the new cognitivist school, which by 1970 was beginning to compete with the expressivist school as the dominant process approach to composition. After all, Janet Emig in her 1971 book *The Composing Processes of Twelfth Graders* had drawn attention not only to the composing processes of writers but also to the mental processes that writers employ while composing. A fierce critic of current-traditional approaches (Crowley, *Composition* 200–01), Emig also established that professional writers as well as students relied on identifiable mental devices and activities that stimulated composition. By the mid-1970s Linda Flower and John R. Hayes at Carnegie Mellon University were studying through a distinctly cognitive lens the composing processes employed by actual writers, students as well as professionals, in an effort to understand empirically the processes involved in composing. Hayes, a psychologist, teamed with Flower to learn more about how the mind tackles the problem of writing. In December of 1977 Flower and Hayes published in *College English* their groundbreaking essay "Problem-Solving Strategies and the Writing Process," a manifesto to their approach to process. They rejected the view of writing as the observance of fixed rules and models and instead called for a more strategic, cognitive "problem-solving" approach: since writing consisted, they felt, of a "hierarchical set of subproblems" tackled iteratively, such as planning and organizing, they offered a set of heuristics to "give the writer self-conscious access to some of the thinking techniques" that good writers use to "generate ideas in language and [. . .] construct those ideas into a written structure" suitable for a specific situation (449, 451). And they were embarking on a research program that would soon generate a series of essays, a 1978 conference, and a set of essays based on that conference, *Cognitive Processes in Writing,* edited by their Carnegie Mellon colleagues Lee Gregg and Erwin Steinberg in 1980. Research by Flower and Hayes was already contributing to pedagogy by broadening instructors' conceptions of the writing process and by enabling instructors to develop "strategies for helping student writers to discover their intentions," including prewriting and inventional strategies, planning and organizational strategies, editing strategies, and so on (Faigley, *Fragments* 30)—all of which were quickly added to pedagogical efforts throughout the nation. Moreover, Flower and Hayes encouraged teachers to understand the writing process as a set of layered cognitive activities involving not just broad activities like "pre-writing" or "revising" but also specific activities practiced by good writers, such as "setting up goals," "finding operators," and "testing your writing against your own editor" ("Problem-Solving" 457–58); in each case Flower and Hayes articulated not only how these strategies worked cognitively but also where they fit into the larger process of writing.

Flower and Hayes were not embraced universally or uncritically (Ann Berthoff, from a position in aesthetics and philosophy, was already especially withering in dismissing what she regarded as the cognitivists' compartmentalization of mental processes); but by 1977 most composition handbooks had come to acknowledge, at least superficially and at most substantially, that writing was a process whose stages ought to be considered in some way by writing teachers—though, as Flower and Hayes pointed out, advocates of process pedagogy tended to take "different roads to the same territory."[16] Most newer textbooks incorporated chapters on invention techniques such as brainstorming and freewriting (products of the expressivists' approach), describing these strategies and providing exercises to guide students through them; and most offered detailed advice about revision as well.

On a final note, as Janice Lauer indicates in her sidebar, one of the key influences on the movement toward process—the reemergence of interest in rhetoric, especially classical rhetoric and rhetorical invention (a development that we discuss later in this chapter)—matured in the second half of the 1960s. Partly because of James Berlin's cat-

Sidebar: Rhetoric and the Process Movement

Janice Lauer

The account of the process movement in *1977* positions it as starting in the 1970s, but I would suggest that it began in the 1960s with a revived interest in rhetoric in the work of Walter Ong, Edward Corbett, Richard Young, Ross Winterowd and others. This interest was further fostered by the formation of the Rhetoric Society of America. I became interested in rhetoric and invention in 1961, when I took two courses from Father Walter Ong in an MA program at St. Louis University. Although the courses were not focused on rhetoric, on the side I read a number of his essays and his recently published, *Ramus, Method, and the Decay of Dialogue,* which detailed the removal of invention from rhetoric in the early Renaissance. Because I was teaching composition at the time, I became curious about the state of invention (if any) in current composition teaching.

egorizing of the expressive and cognitive schools, this influence has been insufficiently acknowledged in accounts of process pedagogies, but the new rhetorical studies were surely not without implications for process-minded scholars and teachers in 1977.

The Impact of Linguistics

Even as the process movement was taking wing, in part under the aegis of breakthroughs in cognitive psychology, other possible solutions to the literacy crisis (some sympathetic to process pedagogy, some more product-oriented) were being supplied by developments in the relatively new and certainly vigorous social science of linguistics.

One such approach to linguistics, "tagmemics," derived from the work of Kenneth Pike and his collaborators at the University of Michigan, Richard Young and Alton Becker.[17] Tagmemics contributed in important ways to the process movement; indeed, Young, Becker, and Pike moved the field into invention, psychology, and cognitive science several years before Flower and Hayes began their own work. In their influential 1970 text *Rhetoric: Discovery and Change,* written even before the publication of Emig's *Composing Processes,* Young, Becker, and Pike defined rhetoric "much more broadly than it had been defined for many years"; they declared that "[rhetoric] is concerned primarily with a creative process that includes all the choices a writer makes from his

When I started my doctoral work at the University of Michigan in 1962, I asked to study rhetoric. I was told by Warner Rice, the legendary chair of English, that they didn't offer rhetoric but that if I followed an alternate route, he would be my advisor. Just as I was planning my dissertation (on the contemporary state of rhetorical invention), I serendipitously met Richard Young at the CCCC; he then was teaching in the engineering school at Michigan. Occasionally we began to dialogue about my interest in invention, his work on tagmemics, and on heuristics in creativity studies. These eventually wove their way into my dissertation, for which he served as a committee member (I finished in 1967). (By the way, at the first Louisville conference, Bob Connors referred to this dissertation as the first in the emerging field of rhetoric and composition and it was used as a text in Richard Young's year-long NEH seminar.)

earliest tentative explorations of a problem in what has been called the 'prewriting' stage of the writing process, through choices in arrangement and strategy for a particular audience, to the final editing of the final draft" (xii). Working from Pike's premise that linguistic action could be understood from the perspectives of particle, wave, and field, and from Young's appropriation of John Dewey's ideas on problem formation in *Logic* and *Democracy and Education,*[18] the authors posed a set of heuristics for examining "units of experience," a category which includes any person, object, or abstraction subject to thought. Much of their textbook consequently offered heuristics for prewriting and invention to help students to solve problems by preparing the mind to understand—and hence to come up with—good material for compositions. But Young, Becker, and Pike also described techniques for examining rhetorical situations (especially for realizing writing as a response to a problem), for editing drafts, and for analyzing texts in preparation for revision. These tactics without question shaped the work of Flower and Hayes and stimulated a great many other process advocates.

But though efforts to ground composition pedagogy and theory in tagmemics proliferated, and though aspects of tagmemic rhetoric reached the classroom through *Rhetoric: Discovery and Change,* through Flower's 1981 textbook *Problem-Solving Strategies for Writ-*

Simultaneously, in my own composition classes and with colleagues I was developing a pedagogy on Writing as a Process of Situated Inquiry, drawing on classical rhetoric, tagmemics, heuristics in creativity, etc. This concept of process conceived of writing as initiated in a situational context (rhetorical situation), which triggers anomalies, puzzles, apparent contradictions or conflicts, a real unknown, that compels the writer to investigate and ultimately to pose a question to guide inquiry. Thus poised with a working question, the writer can widely explore the question and its context, set a working focus and genre for the situation, and write drafts to support and further unpack this unknown. This conception of writing is discussed in several of my scholarly publications (including "Writing as Inquiry: Some Questions for Teachers") and through several editions of *Four Worlds of Writing: Inquiry and Action in Context* (coauthored by me, Andrea Lunsford, Gene Montague, and Janet Emig, and in the fourth

ing, and through J. C. Mathes and Dwight Stevenson's technical writing textbook *Designing Technical Reports,* these efforts never fully surpassed their marginal heuristic applications, possibly because, as Lester Faigley has observed, tagmemics to a degree "failed to account for a variety of distinctions that writers perceived among different texts" (*Fragments* 86). In other words, as a linguistic theory, tagmemics was proving to describe only incompletely the practices of actual speakers and writers. If composition theorists were seeking a model of language use that conformed to students' actual experiences as language users (and which could thus suggest effective strategies for intervening in the writing process), then the analytical strength of linguistic approaches became a detriment when applied to the relatively unsystematic chaos of actual writing. The emergent discipline needed a more comprehensive model to lean on.

This weakness of tagmemics, along with some of its successes, also characterized to a degree one other major linguistic approach to composition of the 1960s and 1970s, transformational-generative (TG) linguistics. In many respects, TG was even more limited than tagmemics in its value for composition and rhetoric in that it was attentive mostly to sentence-level considerations. However, during the 1970s, several rhetorical theorists and compositionists nevertheless aligned themselves with versions of this linguistic current. Several of them,

edition, also by Janet Atwill, Thomas Clemens, Bill Hart-Davidson, Debra Jacobs, Lisa Langstraat, Libby Miles, Tim Peeples, and Nan Uber-Kellogg). Others have also written variously about this concept of Writing as Inquiry, including Richard Young in *Rhetoric: Discovery and Change* and George Hillocks in *College English.*

This work on invention with its entailed view of process contributed to the start of the process movement (an influence that is now buried by the binary of expressive/cognitive); a theory of invention necessarily entails a process conception of writing. Further, this rhetorical conception initiated the writing process *in a context.* This inquiry/context process was circulating through publications, lectures at conventions, and the summer Rhetoric Seminars (which featured through the years theorists such as Richard Young, Ed Corbett, Gordon Rohman, and Janet Emig).

most notably Ross Winterowd and Joseph Williams, sought ways to overcome the limitations of TG by crossing the "sentence boundary" into larger discursive forms, and by uniting it with a broader theory of rhetoric.[19] Furthermore, its contribution to pedagogies like sentence combining and its fundamental role in informing the debates over "students' right to their own language" in the early 1970s made it a significant contributor to new directions in composition.

TG arose from Noam Chomsky's work on the structure of language in the 1950s. Transformational linguists argued that language, in its pure form, is an inherent human capacity, and that language use reflects deep structures in the human mind and in the structure of rationality itself. The transformational linguist's project was to make sense of the complexity of language use by deducing the rules by which the "deep structures" of language become transformed into the "surface structures" evident in actual discourse. In other words, the project involved analysis of how complicated sentences (and, by extension, paragraphs and longer units) were formed from simple, fundamental linguistic structures. The rules governing this transformation from simple to complex (or from fundamental to perceived, or from deep to surface—terminologies vary) comprised the "scientific

Sidebar: Finding Composition

Stephen A. Bernhardt

I arrived at the University of Michigan in 1977, looking for composition. My background as a high school teacher led me to the Joint Interdisciplinary PhD program in English and Education, directed at the time by Stephen Dunning, a poet and a masterful teacher. I knew from teaching high school that I wanted to understand better how to teach writing, and I was interested in English language studies more generally. I was fortunate to arrive just at the time when interest was building in composition and rhetoric, and there were many opportunities to develop a strong program spanning disciplines, departments, and programs.

While there was neither a program nor even a course in composition teaching, the English and Education program was open

laws" of transformational linguistics. Building on the insights of transformational linguistics, compositionists developed a transformational theory of grammar which suggested that the "deep structures" of language use in the human brain were short units of language called "kernel sentences," consisting of discrete combinations of word-groups (such as a subject-verb combination). These kernel sentences were the building blocks of actual discourse, it was believed (though many linguists fought the notion that TG descriptions mirrored actual thought processes and resisted pedagogical applications of TG[20]); and all the rules achieved by TG described either the nature of these kernels or the various transformations to which they could be subjected.

From the mid-1960s well into the 1970s, compositionists increasingly drew upon the insights of TG to teach students the structures of language, intending that this theoretical knowledge would promote the better use of language. Many teachers and textbooks discarded the traditional descriptive terms for sentences—simple, compound, complex, compound-complex—for new linguistic accounts of sentence dy-

to student interests, and the mix of graduate students were all concerned with writing, reading, and literacy issues. Teacher education was at the core of our work, and most of us had experience as teachers in public schools, so we worked within models of language arts that integrated reading, writing, speaking, and listening. Our seminar in the teaching of English attended formally to composition scholarship, among other subjects. We had weekly bag lunch seminars ("Chalk and Cheese") that allowed us to share current interests around a range of projects. Students further along in the program were pushing toward dissertations in composition: John Shafer was working from a text linguistics perspective and introduced me to London School linguistics, functional sentence perspective, and reading research. Barry Kroll was writing on approaches to error, and Irv Hashimoto was refining approaches to teaching writing. Earlier grads—Lee Odell, Ann Gere, Geneva Smitherman, Gary Salvner—had left a legacy of interests in composition and language studies. Students in my cohort group included Patti Stock, Amy Devitt, and Christine Hult; we were all excited by the growing status of composition studies within the university.

namics and terms like "noun phrase," "verb phrase," and "transformations." Linguists and quasi-linguists (not all of them transformationalists to be sure) were very well represented at the major conferences in the field. Perhaps the best-known products of TG's influence on composition were the "generative rhetoric" of Francis Christensen (a sentence-and-paragraph pedagogy based on the cumulative sentence) and sentence combining (a technique that reflected both TG's analytical flavor and its preferred unit, the sentence).[21]

Christensen himself, a professor of English at the University of Southern California, was unaware of the intricacies of transformational-generative linguistics, and "thought of himself as a rhetorician or stylist, rather than a linguist" (Crowley, "Linguistics" 494). Nevertheless, during the 1960s he devised a pedagogy that accommodated the new linguistics. On the basis of his study of seventeenth-century English prose stylists and his sense that the cumulative sentence was especially important in effective current American prose, Christensen had students expand sentences through the use of free modifiers; he

The students in English and Ed shared interests, professors, and classes with a very active Doctor of Arts program. Under the leadership of Alan Howes and Jay Robinson, students like Barbara Couture, John Beard, John Brockmann, and John Reiff were all studying writing in academic and work settings, finding ways to put together individualized programs that drew upon their teaching backgrounds and contributed to theoretical and research based approaches in writing classrooms.

In the English department, much of our work in composition was practice-based, centered on teaching first-year writing. When I arrived, the first-year writing course was a free-for-all, with grad students, primarily students of literature, teaching sections based on their own interests: polite essays, science fiction, contemporary or popular literature, humanistic psychology. Bernard van't Hul, a medievalist, was pulled from his lexicographical work on the *Middle English Dictionary* and made composition director. Bernie was an inspired choice: passionate, affable, well spoken, deeply attuned to the workings of language. Under Bernie, a leadership team of faculty and students was formed to direct the first-year writing program. I was lucky enough to be chosen, in part because during my first year as a teaching assistant, I had shown enthu-

suggested that students might expand paragraphs in an analogous way, noting how writers often expand paragraphs by means of coordinate and subordinate structures; and he promulgated his ideas in his posthumously published *Notes toward a New Rhetoric* (1976), which collected his 1960s essays on his approach. Christensen was subsequently criticized for providing structures that were mostly applicable to narrative and descriptive prose (perhaps unfairly criticized, since cumulative sentences need not be descriptive or narrative) and for providing an analysis that was inadequate to the variety in paragraphs. A. M. Tibbetts responded to the publication of *Notes toward a New Rhetoric* by complaining that this new rhetoric ignored many of the things considered most important to rhetorical effectiveness—defining issues, recognizing logical shortcomings, supporting generalizations (143–44). But Christensen's ideas were nonetheless incorporated into any number of textbooks—at least until sentence combining seemed to offer an even more comprehensive pedagogy, one that promised to encourage

siasm and engagement with pedagogy. My high school teaching background also gave me credible ethos.

Under Bernie's direction, first-year writing was reconceptualized on rhetorical foundations, emphasizing the importance of medium, audience, purpose, and situation (Bernie's MAPS acronym) as a heuristic for understanding how language works and what writers should be thinking about. We intentionally stopped using the term *essay* as an all-purpose word to describe what students write, preferring the term *text,* and we emphasized the need for students to gain experience at analyzing and writing various sorts of texts, differently configured under the MAPS rubric. Bernie was a language maven, and he brought to the program a wide range of texts: legal, sports, biographical, scientific, sociological. We worked through a fair amount of resistance from the English grad students, who resented our taking away their permission to teach with total freedom. Many were not comfortable thinking about texts from various fields of discourse as opposed to the literary works that better represented their interests and expertise.

In 1978, attention to composition was given a huge boost at Michigan by the establishment of the English Composition Board, with large initiating grants from the Mellon and Ford

the advances in sentence production that Christensen had been seeking for a decade.

The objective of sentence combining was not necessarily to discover the fundamental rules of language (as it was for TG itself), but rather to help students to become better at writing complicated (or "syntactically mature") sentences. Teachers who subscribed to sentence combining believed that students would enhance their stylistic sophistication not through studying sentences written by others but through repeated practice in generating and rearranging short kernel sentences into various syntactic patterns. In the words of Sharon Crowley, adherents believed that such practice "might not only reinforce students' native sense of which patterns were structurally sound in English; it might also accelerate their achievement of mastery over more complex patterns" ("Linguistics" 490).

Preliminary research in the 1960s and early 1970s had tested the effects of sentence combining, most importantly John Mellon's 1967 and 1969 grammar studies and Frank O'Hare's 1971 dissertation on

foundations. The ECB was a multi-pronged response to the broad concerns about student literacies that were current in the culture at large. It was exhilarating to enter a well-funded initiative and to help develop and implement writing assessment for placement of entering students, first-year tutorials for those students who needed extra attention, a writing center, outreach to high schools, writing-intensive courses in the disciplines, and workshops for faculty across the disciplines. The same rhetorical framework informed ECB and FYC—an emphasis on the varieties of English in and outside the academy and a real attempt to enlarge the rhetorical framework for understanding language.

Michigan had always had a strong Department of Language and Literature, and the language interests served the interests of composition well. Richard W. Bailey, my mentor and dissertation director, taught a proseminar in English language studies that covered topics in lexicography, syntax, rhetoric, composition, discourse analysis, English as a world language, and other topics. The sense of relevance of studies in language and composition was heightened by the unfolding Ann Arbor Black English case, where Bailey contributed testimony. (He also provided expert testimony in the Patti Hearst case on the question of whether she authored

the growth of syntactic maturity among students trained in sentence combining. William Strong's textbook *Sentence Combining: A Composing Book* appeared in 1973. Then in 1976 and 1977, Donald Daiker and linguists Max Morenberg and Andrew Kerek at Miami University in an elaborate experimental study confirmed that a first-year required writing course that focused exclusively on sentence combining could yield more effective and "syntactically more mature writing" from students than a traditional course based on the modes of discourse (41). They also began work on a sentence combining textbook, *The Writer's Options,* that appeared commercially in 1978 and that was widely adopted. Indeed, even critics of sentence combining agreed that the technique clearly seemed to help students to develop syntactic fluency, and nearly everyone appreciated the substitution of sentence combining for the formal and prescriptive teaching of grammar that usually accompanied current-traditionalism. However, as those critics were pleased to point out, sentence combining did not necessarily help students to understand why they should want to pursue syntactic

the press releases attributed to her on behalf of the Symbionese Liberation Army. Here was stylistic analysis in action!) Campus visitors, some in connection with ECB and some English department guests, included Roman Jakobsen, Dick Ohmann, Ginnie Redish, Jim Kinneavy, James Sledd, Stanley Fish, and Ed Corbett. It was a period of exciting intellectual ferment, a time when interests in language, writing, and rhetoric coalesced.

The campus at large was an important site for interdisciplinary collaboration. In Engineering Humanities, Dwight Stevenson and J. C. Mathes were helping define technical communication as a discipline, stressing an audience-based, rhetorical approach in their influential textbook and in their summer workshops for practicing teachers. Tom Huckin and Leslie Olsen were also part of the Engineering College and, together with Larry Selinker of Linguistics, led interdisciplinary seminars on scientific and technical discourse analysis. The English Language Institute was a site of interdisciplinary work on English as a second language, where the theory and practice of communicative competence were replacing earlier emphases on formal audio-lingual methodology. ELI also did groundbreaking work in defining and teaching the advanced competencies necessary for academic writing and speak-

complexity—why complex sentences were better able to express their meaning. While the approach was a fine analytical and creative tool for improving sentencing, it seemed useful primarily in editing troublesome drafts and tended to detract from interest in planning, invention, arrangement, and other rhetorical considerations.[22]

As with tagmemics, TG was good at simplifying and organizing language, but at the expense of a comprehensive picture of language in its actual use. TG may have seemed attractive to compositionists because of its scientific view of language, as well as its apparent success in producing rational linguistic rules, just the sort of rules one might wish to teach students who were struggling to become competent language users. TG succeeded as a linguistic project, however, not because it provided great insight on how actual writers produced writing, but rather because it explained how language itself operated to yield writing. TG ultimately was interested neither in sociological phenomena (such as the function of writing in real settings) nor in the human problems of producing texts. "Generative grammar" was

ing in university settings. This work was conducted within the framework of English for Special Purposes.

In Linguistics, the tagmemic legacy of Young, Becker, and Pike was strongly felt at Michigan. Richard Young had recently left for Carnegie Mellon, but Alton "Pete" Becker was teaching packed courses on language and culture from an anthropological linguistics perspective. Ken Pike was working with the Linguistic Society of America, where culturally contextualized translation was stressed, seeing units of meaning (tagmemes) as carrying both linguistic and cultural context, both form and meaning, as the smallest unit of analysis. (LSA was busy with the large project of getting the *Bible* translated into as many languages as possible; translating a parable such as the "workers in the vineyard" was obviously not a matter of word-for-word translation but of finding meaningful cultural correlatives.) In Speech Communication, Rich Enos was offering seminars in historical and contemporary rhetoric to appreciative students from English, linguistics, and communication studies. In Education, Loren Barritt was exploring phenomenological approaches to language and thought, while Karen Wixon was pursuing innovative approaches to reading, with interests in literacy.

generative in a severely limited sense—it was concerned with the incidentally human process of generating complex from simple linguistic structures, and not with the human struggle to communicate.[23] (It would be the job of sociolinguistics—then well advanced under the intellectual leadership of Dell Hymes, William Labov, and others—to address those shortcomings: see Jordan.) To put it another way, TG was rather purely scientific and analytical, concerned with breaking down complex texts that already existed and not really with discovering how texts ought to be assembled in the first place. This drawback did not impede TG's value for linguists or current traditionalists, but it limited to a great extent its utility as a grounding for a comprehensive theory of composition. For that it was persistently criticized by Ann Berthoff, who railed against linguistics as a pedagogical source for composition.

Overall, my time at Michigan, beginning in 1977, was made rich by an interdisciplinary community of scholars and teachers focused on language learning. It was important that so many of us saw ourselves as teachers and pursued interests in language learning in all its forms. Composition had yet to emerge as a course, much less a discipline, and we had to travel to Speech Comm to find a course in rhetoric (where they weren't sure how to fit Enos's historical scholarship into a department that was more concerned with television and theater). Because the culture at large had turned its attention to issues of reading and writing, the university was following, with the support of foundations. I found at Michigan an opportunity to gain experience and skills that have served me well throughout my career: helping direct a writing program, spending summers reading assessment essays, determining how to build writing-intensive courses for underprepared first-year students as well as students in the disciplines, and learning to teach English as a second language. I was fortunate to be exposed to programs that valued language in all its varieties, and especially to find encouragement to explore in my dissertation situated technical and scientific writing practices in labs, field stations, and government agencies. The year 1977 was a lucky one for me, a year of induction into the emerging field of rhetoric and composition.

The success of linguistic and sociolinguistic theory, however, played an important role in a key language debate that developed in the mid-1970s, marked most memorably by the publication of NCTE's "Students' Right to Their Own Language" statement in 1976.[24] Linguistics and sociolinguistics had proven to be a powerful tool for detecting and describing the structure of various languages and dialects, and the discovery that all such languages and dialects were structurally integral and even equivalent challenged longstanding assumptions that certain languages (i.e., Western languages like English, French, and German) were inherently superior, more rational, more expressive than other languages and dialects. As a result, rationalizations for purifying students (especially among ethnic and cultural minorities) of their own languages and dialects, under the banner of the movement for "the basics" of standard written English, particularly for the new stu-

Sidebar: Linguistics and Composition

Lester Faigley

One major difference between composition studies in 1977 and in the early twenty-first century is the declining influence of linguistics. In 1977 no one held a PhD in rhetoric and composition. Some people in the emerging field were fortunate to have had some training in rhetoric, but all came to composition from elsewhere, primarily literary studies. Until the 1970s, however, large English departments typically included linguists, who frequently were involved in administering writing programs. Issues involving linguistics were prominent in debates over "correctness" versus "usage" in the 1950s and early 1960s—debates that took on new intensity when sociolinguists argued that "standard" dialects are not inherently superior but gain their status by being spoken by the most powerful groups in a society. In the 1960s linguistics contributed two important lines of scholarship and teaching: the tagmemics theory advanced by Richard Young and Alton Becker, and generative rhetoric proposed by Francis Christensen.

But composition studies missed out on the early impact of Noam Chomsky's theory of transformational grammar, which,

dents now coming to universities, met with opposition that was bolstered by the insights of transformational linguistics and sociolinguistics (e.g., William Labov's *Language in the Inner City* was published in 1972). Stephen Parks has analyzed this moment as "a complicated negotiation between social activists [stemming from the political movements of the late 1960s, including Black Power] and writing teachers attempting to translate a new morality into the classroom" (11). As Geneva Smitherman has noted, "there was a good deal of excitement about the 'New Grammar,' and linguistics seemed to hold out great promise to resolve a whole host of problems in [. . .] the teaching of literacy" ("CCCC's Role" 351). Consequently, the CCCC Executive Committee in 1972 created a committee to draft a document that would be attentive to the implications of linguistics for the teaching of composition, especially to students on the margins. The ultimate result was "Students' Right to Their Own Language," a 1974 resolution and subsequent 1976 publication that challenged teachers to attend to the implications of the new linguistics. A product of the scholarship and collaboration on the part of Smitherman, Elisabeth McPherson, Richard Lloyd-Jones, Ross Winterowd, and others, "Students' Right" was designed "(1) to heighten consciousness of language attitudes; (2) to promote the value of linguistic diversity; and (3) to convey facts and information about language and language variation that would enable

despite Chomsky's protests to the contrary, inspired a great deal of research across social science disciplines. Chomsky's work came to composition studies through the efforts of Kellogg Hunt on syntactic development in the 1960s. Hunt's suggestion that sentence combining practice would enhance the syntactic maturity of developing writers was demonstrated in several studies with junior-high-age children, most notably by John Mellon and Frank O'Hare. In 1977 Donald Daiker, Andrew Kerek, and Max Morenberg published the results of a major study at Miami University, which concluded that a sentence combining curriculum could increase the syntactic maturity and overall writing quality of first-year college students.

It is difficult looking back today to sense how much excitement this study produced: for the first time, there was irrefutable proof that a well-defined writing curriculum could produce measurable results. Sentence combining was not the total answer,

instructors to teach their non-traditional students—and ultimately all students—more effectively" (Smitherman, "CCCC's Role" 359).

Objections to the statement were immediate, and spirited defenses of teaching standard English continued to appear in books and journals during the late 1970s, the most eloquent such defense, perhaps, found in an early chapter in E. D. Hirsch's *The Philosophy of Composition* (1977). But equally eloquent and more linguistically sophisticated were reasoned defenses of the linguistic competence of marginalized groups, especially African Americans. Smitherman's 1977 *Talkin' and Testifyin,'* a landmark study of the elements, origins, and development of Black English that offers one sharp counterpart to *The Philosophy of Composition* (there were many others), refuted allegations that the dialect used by urban African Americans was somehow illogical or substandard or reflective of diminished linguistic ability in its users. The book not only traced the development of Black English from its slave origins to the 1970s, but it urged teachers of writing and speech to acknowledge and legitimate the linguistic communities from which African American students were coming. By advocating a "greater concept of language" and by focusing on students' writing processes, "initially ignor[ing] issues of correctness and dialect, instructors would be able to make the students' experience of primary importance" (Parks 124, 153). *Talkin' and Testifyin'* praised the "Students' Right" statement and closed with a challenge to teachers "to struggle for a national public policy on language which would reassert the legitimacy of languages other than English, and American dialects other than standard" (241). At a historical moment when ethnic and cultural minorities in particular were entering the university, the outcome of the "Students' Right" controversy had the potential to impact the conduct of composition and indeed of modern education, especially through the pedagogy of "basic writing" classes, where many second-language speakers as well

but it carried the promise that the complexity of writing could be analyzed and taught effectively. Major breakthroughs seemed to be on the immediate horizon. In the three decades since 1977, not only has the prominence of linguistics declined within composition studies, but also the optimism it carried.

as speakers of non-standard dialects tended to find themselves. But of course critics remained unconvinced and respectful of the value of Edited American English; they frequently expressed worries about the prospects for economic advancement for students who had not mastered standard English.

In fact, even among those willing to accept the linguists' claims for linguistic relativism and to value nonstandard dialects, debates about pedagogy arose. Proponents of "bi-dialectalism" (or "biloquialism"), the view that speakers of nonstandard dialects needed to learn how to speak "standard English" for pragmatic reasons, accepted the linguistic value of nonstandard dialects in principle but argued that upward social and economic mobility was dependent on the ability to "switch codes," to adopt the standard dialect of the upwardly mobile, in public contexts (the academy, the business world, and the political realm). Probably the most articulate and vociferous opponent of bi-dialectalism was James Sledd, a compositionist who took up English linguistics in the 1930s and 1940s and whose four NEH seminars in linguistics beginning in the late 1970s (three of them offered in the summer and all collectively entitled "Standard English: Its Nature, History, and Social Functions") prompted four dozen seminarians to explore the role of standard English as a "class dialect" (Sledd, personal correspondence). With reading lists that covered "all of sociolinguistics and much of linguistic history," the seminars considered contemporary debates ranging from the perennial "literacy crises" to the "foofaraw about Ebonics" (Sledd, personal correspondence). In addition to his NEH seminars, Sledd contributed during the 1970s (and later) to debates over linguistics, English pedagogy, and the "literacy crisis" through several important articles that challenged compositionists to examine the basis of their commitments to students and to literacy education. According to Sledd (who of course responded vigorously to Hirsch's *Philosophy of Composition*), most relativist linguists and compositionists were missing the point when they claimed they were simply helping minorities to get ahead in the mainstream world, since this claim depended upon an assumption that "getting ahead" (in the sense of upward social and economic mobility) was an inherent good, the obvious goal of language learning for all people. While he never objected to teaching standard English to those who wished to learn it, Sledd argued vigorously against compulsory bi-dialectalism on pragmatic and moral grounds, calling it "open-eyed hypocrisy" to claim that all dialects were equally legitimate while compelling instruction in standard English (Sledd, "English for Survival" 74; "Bi-Dialectalism" 33).

Linguistics, then, provided something of a mixed bag of theoretical resources for the field of composition in the 1970s. It supported defenses of nonstandard dialects and their speakers and influenced developments toward less formal, error-oriented pedagogies. At the same time, it left room for pedagogical stances which sought to indoctrinate speakers of nonstandard dialects into the "class dialect" of standard English, with its attendant norms and values. And it was amenable to being appropriated by current traditionalists.

Basic Writing and Writing Centers

Even as transformational-generative grammar and tagmemics were providing a new, "scientific" approach to teaching, then, English departments were finding themselves teaching a so-called "new breed" of student in the late 1970s, students for whom "a right to their own language" was particularly applicable. Before 1977, students whose prior education had not sufficiently prepared them for freshman-level composition were placed in "remedial" classes that typically stressed correctness and standard English; the designers of those courses hoped that students would learn, succeed, and eventually graduate, but if students failed those classes and dropped out, nothing much seemed lost. The remedial course, like many of the standard required composition courses offered on many campuses, functioned as a gatekeeper, as a de facto "instrument of exclusion" (Crowley, "Response" 89); it was "part of the undemocratic tracking system pervading American mass education, an added layer of linguistic control to help manage some disturbing economic and political conditions on campus" (Shor 93). However, with practical worries about retention and lost tuition dollars, with growing educational concerns for the literacy of the "new" students, and with a social concern for the success of the new students in an academic environment, a new approach to underprepared college students was clearly necessary. While Ira Shor today understands basic writing as part of a "field of control to manage the time, thought, aspirations, composing, and credentials of millions of non-elite students," at the time basic writing was being invented, many teachers were drawn to it as a liberatory pedagogy, as an idealistic effort to help the new students to become integrated into university environments and to increase their chances of flourishing and graduating (93).

Gary Tate's 1976 book, *Teaching Composition: Ten Bibliographic Essays,* was among the first to include a call for an improved curriculum for the new students that were filling the universities. Mina Shaughnessy's essay in Tate's book outlined pedagogical strategies after bemoaning the dearth of research that had left teachers "without an accumulation of published information [about] the new students. [. . . W]e are left with a highly circumscribed literature, essentially the bits and pieces of information that make their way back from the frontier" ("Basic Writing"192). Shaughnessy's own 1977 *Errors and Expectations* was the most comprehensive subsequent response to this demand for research and pedagogy suited to basic writers, those who had performed poorly on college placement exams or non-traditional students who had been out of school long enough to require a refresher course to prepare them for college-level work. Using the close examination of student writing to research error and to recommend changes to the curriculum, Shaughnessy worked to understand the nature of error and the logic lying behind it. Convinced that "basic" writers were able thinkers and persuaded by the insights of the new linguistics that the number of errors in their papers stemmed not from any lack of ability but from lack of practice—"The beginning writer does not know how writers behave" (*Errors,* 13)—she suggested that instructors look for *types* of error and from these seek out a pedagogy to attack patterns of error. Her pedagogy for working with students combined the cognitive, affective, linguistic, and behavioral aspects of writing (though not especially the rhetorical or social aspects[25]) in order to serve better the students of CUNY (see her "Diving In"). And her research offered numerous concrete suggestions to the many instructors who in 1977 were faced with basic writers but had little information about how to meet their needs.

Shaughnessy was certainly not alone as a concerned instructor of basic writers. Many dedicated teachers stuck stubbornly to approaches rooted in current-traditionalism, assigning skills-and-drills exercises more than naturalistic essays; some of these criticized Shaughnessy either for being too sympathetic with poorly prepared students who were too lazy to deserve college or for being insufficiently critical of the social and educational structures that were producing such students. But many others were inquiring into the nature of the problem, experimenting with newer approaches, and sharing the results of those experiments. The *Journal of Basic Writing*, edited by Shaughnessy, quickly attracted a number of contributors who were together focusing on underprepared students. Walter Ong's work on orality and literacy—his *Interfaces of the Word* appeared in 1977—was beginning to be appropriated by teachers who felt that the linguistic behavior of basic writers could be explained by their dependence on oral formulations. Ideas were also borrowed from the new discipline of English as a Second Language in the belief that many basic writers were in fact picking up a new language or dialect.

Andrea Lunsford at Ohio State University was also initiating research to help understand the needs of basic writers and to assess the best approaches in working with them. While Shaughnessy called for a clearer understanding of the stages of growth in one's writing ability as well as a means by which to teach subskills, an understanding which would be enhanced through a knowledge of Piaget's research on how children think as well as other developmental models, Lunsford in her 1977 dissertation ("An Historical, Descriptive, and Evaluative Study of Remedial English in American Colleges and Universities") reflected upon her actual experiences working with basic writers at Ohio State. Thrown somewhat unexpectedly into the job of offering basic writing instruction (perhaps because she had taught high school and had a good sense of the students who needed basic writing instruction) and energized by a three-day visit that Mina Shaughnessy made to Ohio State during the 1975–76 academic year (to this day Lunsford remembers Shaughnessy as "mesmeric," "hypnotic," and "personally magnetic"), Lunsford laid aside her plans for a dissertation on Alexander Bain in favor of a consideration of basic writing. She and Sara Garnes during the 1976–77 academic year piloted a basic writing course that capitalized on what people in two-year colleges and in the Bay Area Writing Project had learned about poorly prepared students; they added insights from psychology to explain basic writing behaviors and to develop testing instruments, especially ones related to attitudes (Lunsford, personal interview). Because of the gathering prestige of the Ohio State program in composition (led by Edward P. J. Corbett and Susan Miller[26]), and because Shaughnessy was busy as a consultant to other New York City campuses through regular Saturday lunches with people like Donald McQuade, Harvey Wiener, and Kenneth Bruffee,

Shaughnessy's influence spread rapidly even before the appearance of *Errors and Expectations* (Lunsford, personal interview).

What Shaughnessy and Lunsford and many of those other concerned researchers were calling for was an emphasis on skills, including not only grammatical ability but also reading and writing. Most basic writers' work demonstrated a lack of planning in composition, an over-attention to fine-tuning (grammatical correctness), and a lack of conceptual complexity. To address these general issues, instructors needed to be trained in linguistics, composition theory, and learning theory. One version of the new basic writing classroom emphasized writing as a process, allowing time for multiple drafts and peer review. Another, more formal approach (implied by *Errors and Expectations*) concentrated on the smaller units of paragraphs or sentences: students practiced effective construction of paragraphs, sentence by sentence. Students might work on writing paragraphs of different types (description, narration, illustration, etc.) throughout the entire semester, focusing on presenting coherent ideas in a single paragraph. Though there was still no one prevailing definition of "the" basic writing course, no single "standard" version of it, basic writing courses, particularly when their focus was on breaking down composition into "skills" more easily managed by underprepared writers, were meant to alleviate the perceived need among entering college students suggested by "Why Johnny Can't Write."

Writing centers were developing along similar lines to meet the requirements of underprepared students and others working to negotiate the demands of academic discourse. Though writing centers, or writing "clinics" or "labs," had developed in the 1940s and 1950s, what they had to offer seemed particularly applicable in the 1970s, with all of its attention to basic writers. Increasingly, therefore, writing centers were developing, expanding and growing in sophistication to alleviate the demands placed on instructors as more and more composition students entered the university, as more and more instructors found their classes growing larger, and as more and more part-time and graduate student instructors were hired. To relieve pressure and to offer specialized instruction, writing center staff could meet regularly with students and make concerted efforts to improve their writing bit by bit. Writing centers, like the one at the University of Iowa under the leadership of Lou Kelly, answered to the student need for one-on-one work and to the need on various campuses for a high profile intellectual center for issues related to writing: for basic writers especially, this individualized attention was meant to complement the help they received in the classroom. Sometimes writing centers experimented with relatively inexpensive technologies associated with language learning—headsets, audiotapes, and workbooks were developed to permit students to learn independently, especially to eliminate grammatical errors—but most often the machines were discarded in favor of human teachers, especially when critics scorned the programmed learning materials and the current-traditional assumptions behind them (Veit). Individualized, human attention was particularly appropriate to address students at their various levels of preparation and to offer them assistance in reaching the standards expected of all university students. These very concerns led to the opening of a writing center at the University of Wyoming in 1977, for example. The leaders of the center noted "that the university has a moral obligation to offer [. . .] a real means of assistance to the students it admits who are likely to fail Freshman English because of inadequate educational background [and] that there is no basis for believing that remedial courses could provide this assistance for an acceptable percentage of the students required to take the course" (Warnock and Eggers 8).[27]

Most often, tutors in the writing center were composition instructors who understood clearly the expectations held for basic writers in the classroom. However, there was also a movement beginning in the 1970s to use peer tutors in writing centers, on economic grounds and in the belief that students would be more comfortable working with other students. "Training and Using Peer Tutors," by Paula Beck, Thom Hawkins, and Marcia Silver, presented at NCTE in 1977 and published in *College English* in 1978, reported the use of peer tutors at Nassau Community College, Brooklyn College, and Cal–Berkeley; all three were taking cues from Kenneth Bruffee, who had been making progress at Brooklyn College with peer tutors and collaborative learning in the writing center since 1972. Regardless of whether they employed peers, graduate students, or faculty members as tutors, writing centers typically employed individualized instruction, often in weekly, half-hour long meetings between tutor and student. Students could set the agenda, seeking assistance for their specific concerns, and this focused instruction increased students' enthusiasm and hopes for success. In his introduction to *Writing Centers: Theory and Administration* (1984, edited by Gary A. Olson), Thom Hawkins discusses the many positive attributes of the writing center, especially collaborative learning, citing the value of "the redesign of the learning environment so that more of the responsibility and the activity of learning is shifted onto the learner. There is a sharing of power, accompanied by the recognition that, since we are all learners, we are all capable of being teachers and that teaching and learning are complementary activities" (xii).

The values evident in the basic writing classroom and in writing centers were also apparent in the various "writing projects" that were springing up in the mid-1970s. These writing projects encouraged the development of a "peer learning community" by bringing together high school teachers and college instructors who could share their experiences in the classroom, and, through their mutual inquiry, who could uncover successful methods of teaching writing. Teachers teaching teachers: here was an example of peer learning that could be replicated in the classroom when students were encouraged to help each other with their writing. The Bay Area Writing Project, begun by high school teacher James Gray in 1973 in conjunction with the University of California at Berkeley, initiated the movement. As Harvey Daniels

Sidebar: The Birth of WAC

Elaine Maimon

The December 8, 1975, issue of *Newsweek,* with the cover story on "Why Johnny Can't Write," had a direct impact on the Arcadia University (née Beaver College) writing program. The dean summoned me to his office and threw the magazine at me. Now, that's impact in its literal sense. I was a first-year, untenured assistant professor, so, of course, I was also Director of Composition.

The MLA meeting later that month turned out to be a turning point in my professional life and the beginning of writing across the curriculum at Beaver College. In a San Francisco ballroom, I heard Mina Shaughnessy sound the call in her speech entitled "Diving In," one that inspired me and so many others to believe that the teaching of writing was worthy of the highest intellectual and scholarly investment. Immediately after Shaughnessy's

and Steven Zemelman note in the introduction to their *A Writing Project* (1985), "the founders of the Bay Area Writing Project believed that teachers who were given the opportunity to write, to share their work with colleagues, to study recent composition theory and research, to reexamine their own classroom practices, and to develop their own plans for improved instruction would become more effective writing teachers" (3). Many other writing projects quickly arose in imitation of the Bay Area project, including the Huntington Beach Writing Project (under the leadership of Ross Winterowd), and they were eventually subsumed under the auspices of a National Writing Project. The writing projects focused mainly on the values of process pedagogy, writing across the curriculum, and peer editing, as well as the ideas of writing to learn and writing to a particular audience with a particular purpose. The projects professed a belief in the power of writing as an enjoyable activity, and their leaders set out to improve teachers both as classroom mentors and as writers. To some extent composition courses housed in English departments remained insulated from the pedagogical excitement generated by the writing projects, which were typically the product of collaboration among high school teachers and university English education specialists; but in many cases the projects did in-

speech, on a San Francisco cable car, I met Harriet Sheridan, the Acting President of Carleton College. I returned home a few days later with the Carleton Plan—a proposal for cross-disciplinary faculty workshops on the teaching of writing.

Fast-forward to July 14, 1977, when Beaver College received from the National Endowment for the Humanities (NEH) the largest federal grant ever received to that date in the history of the College, "A Program to Strengthen the Humanities at Beaver College through an Emphasis on Instruction in Writing and Reading by All Faculty." During that same summer, NEH also provided funding to create the National Writing Project from the seeds sown in the Berkeley-Bay Area. Until then, NEH did not consider writing as part of the humanities. 1977 was the year that the U.S. government, through NEH, recognized writing as transcending narrow definitions and encompassing thinking and learning across the curriculum.

vigorate composition programs and individual composition teachers in university English departments as well.

In keeping with the suggestions of basic skills researchers, writing centers and writing projects offered the perfect opportunity to research underprepared writers, this time in individualized and small-group settings. In addition to this valuable resource, writing centers, writing projects, and basic writing courses helped to satisfy the demands of a concerned public and a growing number of students. More broadly, writing centers and basic writing courses could be open to all students at a university, thereby strengthening the writing connections throughout the university and college curriculum.

Writing Across the Curriculum

Yet another response to the perceived deficiency in student writing and thinking abilities in the 1970s, Writing Across the Curriculum (WAC) programs were designed to connect writing to other disciplines. They sought to strengthen the so-called content areas of the curriculum through the expanded and self-conscious use of writing; in the bargain, students' writing abilities would also improve. As David Russell has detailed in *Writing in the Academic Disciplines, 1870–1990: A Curricular History,* the WAC movement in some respects can be traced to developments in Britain in the 1960s and 1970s, which responded to "compartmentalization" by focusing on language as central to all learning. In the United States during the middle and late 1970s, education journals began to call for a more general educational focus in the university, general education allowing for greater interconnections than the movement toward specialization in the professions did. The specialization endemic to the modern American university was generating counter-efforts in the direction of general education that inevitably involved writing. In 1977, Janet Emig published "Writing as a Mode of Learning," an article that drew on the theories of Vygotsky, Piaget, Dewey, and Bruner; from these developmental theories, she concluded that writing has a "unique value for learning" any subject (122). Because students were becoming too specialized, educators began to emphasize the value of demonstrating writing proficiency in a variety of genres or professional settings. The classroom was to become more of a community, and, with connections to writing across disciplines, more of a linking force within the university as a whole. Another focus of WAC was on the students themselves, on student-centered learning. Being aware of the discourse conventions in one's field was seen as vital to one's academic and professional success, and producing students with the ability to write was a goal that everyone could subscribe to. So too, Writing Across the Curriculum could help answer to the members of the various disciplines who complained that first-year composition was not preparing students sufficiently for work in other courses and in the workplace after graduation. Including writing in all courses would make writing instruction the responsibility of the university as a whole, and the importance placed on writing would thus be clearly apparent to every student.

Some of these assumptions were already being put into practice in 1977, most notably by Elaine Maimon at Beaver College in Pennsylvania and by Art Young, Toby Fulwiler, and their colleagues at Michigan Technological University. Maimon, who was awarded an NEH grant in 1977 to design a comprehensive WAC program at Beaver College, focused on writing to learn via process pedagogy and collaborative learning, both techniques meant to bring together the university as a community. Out of her experience came one of the first WAC textbooks, *Writing in the Arts and Sciences* (1981). Just as influential, however, was the work being done at Michigan Tech, where Young, Fulwiler, and others brought together faculty from various disciplines for elaborate, extended, inventive writing workshops that helped the instructors incorporate writing into their courses in new and effective ways. Fulwiler emphasized journal writing across the curriculum, valuing the mechanisms of journal writing, and dialogue, and focusing on the writing process rather than finished products. In all WAC programs, however, writing was viewed as a medium for general intellectual development: WAC courses were meant to promote general literacy, critical thinking, improved writing, and active learning. The overall goal was to improve writing in all content areas of the curriculum: students could both "learn to write" and "write to learn." The interconnected nature of WAC programs effectively answered those who were concerned about the quality of student writing at the college level by providing students with additional opportunities to hone their skills throughout their college years.

Technical Writing and Business Writing

Actually, writing across the curriculum programs were not the first to support writing in the disciplines. Business writing and technical writing courses had developed with some sophistication for many years in the nation's colleges of business and engineering. But although technical writing and business writing courses had existed in universities since the first decades of the century, and although technical writing as a profession had developed out of the technological developments associated with World War II, the Cold War, and Taylorism, concerns about literacy in the professions led to a significant increase in demand for technical and business writing in the 1970s. As college enrollments increased and particularly as more and more students flocked to courses in technology, engineering, and business, more students required or elected courses in technical writing or business writing (which were now offered in English departments as well as in business and engineering colleges). And as demand increased—ten percent per year during many of the years of the 1970s (Connors, "Rise of Technical" 347)—so did concerns for teacher preparation and curricular development.[28]

Consequently, in 1973 a group of faculty from several universities, responding to the leadership of Thomas Pearsall at the University of Minnesota, founded the Council for Programs in Technical and Scientific Communication, an effort to share pedagogical information among schools with technical communication programs. In the same year the Association of Teachers of Technical Writing was founded and began producing *The Technical Writing Teacher,* edited by Donald Cunningham, as a forum for new pedagogical work related to technical communication. The teachers who started CPTSC and ATTW were generally interested in wresting technical and business communications from their own kind of current traditionalism: both subdisciplines were struggling to emerge from product-oriented pedagogical traditions that were embedded in positivist attitudes toward language (see Britton), in an emphasis on static forms and formulaic advice, and in an obsession with matters of appearance, usage, and correctness. Accordingly, ATTW encouraged Cunningham and Herman Estrin to develop a collection of essays for beginning teachers that they called *The Teaching of Technical Writing* and that was attentive in some ways to newer approaches to the teaching of writing; and NCTE asked Pearsall, co-author of the widely adopted *Reporting Technical Information* and an expert on audience analysis, to put together a collection called *Teaching Technical Writing: Methods for College English Teachers.* When both collections appeared in 1975, they quickly became influential guides to new teachers of technical writing in many locations, and they tacitly encouraged such teachers away from exclusively product-oriented tactics recommended by textbooks of the 1950s and 1960s. In the mid-1970s, J. C. Mathes and Dwight Stevenson, members of the Humanities Department in the College of Engineering at Michigan (which had sponsored serious thought about technical communication for years), began to direct summer seminars in the teaching of technical writing to college teachers that featured Cunningham, other technical writing experts, and Michigan colleagues like James Zappen, Leslie Olsen, and Thomas Sawyer.[29] (Sawyer's *Technical and Professional Communication: Teaching in the Two-Year College, Four-Year College, and Professional School* emerged in 1977 with early articles by new scholars like Deborah Andrews, Jeanne Halpern, and Carolyn Miller.) Among Mathes and Stevenson's colleagues in their department at Michigan also was Richard Young, who appeared at the summer seminars and whose ideas about the teaching of writing, especially tagmemics, heavily influenced Mathes and Stevenson's widely admired textbook *Designing Technical Reports,* which in 1976 incorporated problem-solving conceptualizations and a full-fledged process approach into the engineering report-writing process. Similar programs for new teachers developed at Rensselaer Polytechnic Institute, where Jay Gould had begun publishing the *Journal of Technical Writing and Communication* in 1970, at Hinds Junior College (under the leadership of Nell Ann Pickett), and at other colleges and universities, six of which were offering summer workshops by 1980 (Staples 158). These seminars prepared serious teachers of technical writing to work in English departments, among them Paul Anderson, who came out of the University of Washington (where he had worked with James Souther, whose *Technical Report Writing* was heavily influenced by the composition pedagogy of Porter Perrin [Souther 6]) and into Miami University in 1976 with a commitment to process pedagogy and problem-solving approaches that were derived from Mathes and Stevenson and that were as new there as they would have been in most places.

Meantime, the American Business Communication Association, under the leadership of Francis Weeks, Arn Tibbetts, and their colleagues at the University of Illinois (where George Burton Hotchkiss had begun business writing classes early in the century—see Weeks—and where intellectual leadership had developed in support of business writing that was akin to the kind exhibited at Michigan for technical writing), expanded significantly in the mid-1970s and assumed the responsibility for preparing teachers for courses in business writing. Roughly half of those courses were offered through English departments nationwide, and half through colleges of business: perhaps owing to the association between business colleges and business writing courses, curricula and pedagogical methods remained quite traditional in business writing through the 1970s. Despite the professional efforts of the people at Illinois, textbooks remained very attentive to rather static common genres (e.g., students were taught formulas for producing various kinds of letters); process-based and rhetorically based business communication courses were quite exceptional across the nation; and Jeanne Halpern's *Teaching Business Writing,* a collection dedicated to promulgating new pedagogies in the tradition of the books developed by Cunningham, Estrin, and Pearsall for technical writing (e.g., the book included a chapter by Linda Flower), appeared only in 1983. Business communication as a subdiscipline throughout the 1970s remained insulated to a degree from the kinds of intellectual and social forces that were animating composition pedagogy nationally.

Rhetoric, the "New Rhetoric," and a New Professionalism

Process pedagogies and pedagogies inspired by developments in linguistics, then, were substantial counters to current-traditionalism in 1977. Other formidable alternatives to current-traditionalism were suggested by people committed to what was known as "the new rhetoric." If Ross Winterowd was associated with linguistics and with the new writing projects, for instance, he was also one of several people associated with the search for a grounding in rhetoric in general—and a "new rhetoric" in particular—that many hoped might produce a solution to the literacy crisis. Daniel Fogarty had encouraged the search for "a new rhetoric" in 1957 with the publication of his *Roots for a New Rhetoric,* a book that proposed a series of possible theoretical groundings for an as-yet-unformulated "new rhetoric" that seemed to be required in America, particularly as a replacement for current-traditionalism (a term which Fogarty invented). Martin Steinmann in 1967 published a collection of essays, *The New Rhetorics,* that had the same general aim. The trouble was, twenty years after Fogarty's book and ten years after Steinmann's, no one could easily agree on which "new rhetoric" would work best.

Linguists, as we have already noted, were considering their subject to be one of the possible grounds for a new rhetoric.[30] But others (including Winterowd, linguist or not, and including Fogarty and Steinmann) were touting the work of Kenneth Burke as a grounds for an invigorated composition curriculum. Even though Burke himself in a 1978 essay in *College Composition and Communication* had discouraged the use of his dramatistic pentad as a tool for writers (he regarded dramatism as a tool for analysts of writing, not producers), William Irmscher was still promoting Burke and dramatism in his widely used *Holt Guide to English* (first published in 1972); and Winterowd's *The Contemporary Writer,* published in 1975, recommended the pentad to student writers as well. In addition, process-movement advocates were finding a place for dramatism within their approach too as an invention heuristic and even as an aid to revision. Witness William Keith's 1977 essay in *CCC,* which described an entire composition course given over to coaching the composing process that is highly attentive to Burke's work, and witness Charles Kneupper's careful study of Burke in Richard Young's NEH seminar (see below), which resulted in his 1979 essay on using Burke to teach invention. In yet another *CCC* essay completed in 1977, Joseph Comprone could state with confidence that "Burke's pentad can be a heuristic basis for disciplined inquiry into all elements of the writing process" (340).

Not that it was only the pentad that people were mining from Burke. Winterowd, for instance, who was onto Burke very early in his career[31] and in a very comprehensive way, was recommending concepts from *The Philosophy of Literary Form* and *Counter-Statement,* especially (but not only) regarding form. Young, Becker, and Pike meanwhile recommended Burke's notions of "perspective by incongruity" as an invention heuristic. John Warnock and Tilly Eggers suggested that *A Rhetoric of Motives* "could provide the background for the whole discussion" of the University of Wyoming composition program's theoretical underpinnings (5). And Edward P. J. Corbett was speaking approvingly of Burke's notion of "identification" (from *A Rhetoric of Motives*) at the end of his *Classical Rhetoric for the Modern Student.* While many people found Burke perplexing and resisted founding their courses on Burkean principles, it is nonetheless clear that many composition teachers in 1977 were applying Burke's principles to their work.

Others, impressed by the work of Chicago School scholars associated with Burke,[32] with pragmatism, and with classical rhetoric—most notably Wayne Booth—were proposing rhetorical and "new rhetorical" methods deriving from a pragmatic neo-Aristotelianism that had been championed at the University of Chicago ever since John Dewey and George Herbert Mead came to the university at its inception in the 1890s and since Richard McKeon arrived in the mid-1930s. People were especially attracted to Booth's work on "rhetorical stance," to the Chicago School's general reinvigoration of classical studies (though most Chicagoans attended far more to Aristotle's *Poetics* than to his *Rhetoric*), and to Richard Weaver's classically-informed work on argument. Booth's articles "The Revival of Rhetoric" (which was included in Steinmann's collection) and "The Rhetorical Stance" (which had appeared in *CCC* in 1963 and which was reproduced in several anthologies and duplicated in many places by composition teachers) stimulated interest in rhetorical approaches to composition in English departments respectful of his groundbreaking *The Rhetoric of Fiction* (1961) and attracted to the reader-oriented practical criticism now coming to the fore under his influence. "The Rhetorical Stance" encouraged people to teach composition students how to balance the shifting claims of writer, audience, and subject and to consider composition as a matter of invention and inquiry rather than a strictly and narrowly verbal art; and he redirected attention to student writing as a rhetorical response to a social exigency. Rhetorically oriented approaches emphasizing audience and situation, appropriateness and flexibility, were obviously anathema to the current traditionalists and to the "authentic voice" pedagogies that had emerged in the 1960s and that were still in place in 1977, and some teachers felt that the rhetorical program was difficult to reconcile with new process pedagogies[33]; but many others were powerfully attracted to the possibilities of the rhetorical pragmatics implied in neo-Aristotelianism. The Chicago School also contributed to the growing (if sometimes vague) dissatisfaction with current-traditionalism because the Chicago School defined itself in part against the arhetorical (even anti-rhetorical) efforts of the New Critics[34]; and it operated pedagogically through a system of staff meetings that became legendary for their stimulating (and sometimes intimidating) conduct and for their ability to create commonalities in instruction across sections.

That Richard Weaver, loosely associated with the Chicago School by virtue of his position on the faculty there from 1944 to 1963,[35] had developed critical essays on classical rhetoric and pedagogies emphasizing argument gave a general boost as well to rhetorically-based, argument-oriented courses, particularly after the posthumous publication of his *Language Is Sermonic* in 1970. Though Weaver is associated with conservative causes today on account of his controversial book *Ideas Have Consequences* and his association with the Southern Agrarians (who, incidentally, should not be understood as easily "conservative" in the way the word is now used—i.e., to denote sympathy with capitalism), and though his work is far more thoroughly neo-Platonic than neo-Aristotelian, Weaver probably deserves to be considered among the New Rhetoricians on account of his contributions to modern rhetorical theory and pedagogy. Weaver studied not just Aristotle and Plato but Cicero and Quintilian, his essays on *The Phaedrus* and other texts domesticated Plato for new rhetoricians, and his essays on argument—recommending Aristotelian topics as an approach to invention in argument (e.g., see Bilsky et al.)—influenced a number of textbook writers and classroom teachers both directly and (as we shall see) indirectly.

Sidebar: Two Gentlemen in Wyoming

Sharon Crowley

In response to a request from Wendy, Brent, and Jack asking me to reflect on the "lines of thought" that produced "Of Gorgias and Grammatology" way back in 1977, I rummaged through my files looking for something, anything, that would jog my memory about its composition. I calculated while searching–ohmigod–that I wrote that piece over twenty-eight years ago! Happily my search produced a letter from Art Simpson, then director of the Wyoming Conference on Freshman and Sophomore English (so states the letterhead), asking me to serve as "an additional consultant" at the 1978 meeting of the conference. The major consultants proposed for that year were Wayne Booth, Walker Gibson, and Stanley Fish. In testament to Art Simpson's professional savvy, each of these thinkers represented a strand of the intellectual interests stirring among teachers of composition at the time, all of which are mentioned in *1977:* Booth a Chicago rhetorical critic; Fish a

The fact that the Chicago School attended so thoroughly to the Greek and Roman classics also contributed to the prestige of classical rhetoric that was gathering around the work of Edward P. J. Corbett at Ohio State. Corbett, having received his MA from Chicago in 1948, had published *Classical Rhetoric for the Modern Student* in 1965 and revised it in 1971; and now in 1977 he was in the midst of a term as editor of *College Composition and Communication.* By the force of his scholarship, energy, personality, and editorial reach and with the help of talented graduate students like Robert Connors, Andrea Lunsford, Gerald Mulderig, Betsy Brown, and John Ruszkiewicz (among others) who were drawn to work with him, Corbett was directing new attention to the classical tradition as well as to eighteenth- and nineteenth-century rhetoricians like Blair, Bain, and Campbell; and he was influencing composition curricula around the country towards neo-classical concepts and assumptions. Not only did those curricula adopt Corbett's approach to teaching style through classical systems of tropes and schemes, but they also accommodated two of the clas-

reader-response theorist, and Gibson associated with the expressivist school of composing then taught at Amherst. One of the great things about the Wyoming Conference, as Art's letter makes clear, was that consultants were asked to be "reasonably available as a resource person to the conference," which meant, in practice, that Booth, Gibson, and Fish hobnobbed all week long with the rest of the conferees at sessions, at barbecues and sing-alongs, and at dances at the Cowboy Bar in downtown Laramie.

I was not working with any of the "lines of thought" represented by the major consultants at Wyoming that year. I became interested in the history of rhetoric while I was in graduate school, and during the early 1970s I read Ong and Howell and Kennedy as well as the work of scholars in speech communication who were putting together a history of modern rhetorical theory–Bevilacqua, Ehninger, Wallace, and others. And then in 1976 something wonderfully fortuitous occurred—my friend and colleague, Bryan Short, took a sabbatical at Yale. Derrida was teaching there that year, and Bryan came back to work all fired up about deconstruction. He insisted that we read Derrida together, and four of us formed a reading group. We called ourselves the Post-Structuralist Luncheon Club, and we met weekly for several years thereafter, at

sical rhetoricians' other key canons for writing: invention (what some of the process advocates had been calling "pre-writing") and arrangement. Corbett's work in the 1970s was congruent with the work of many rhetoricians in speech communications departments who were advancing classical rhetoric in several directions and who were in the vanguard of promoting the "new rhetoric." Most compositionists were insulated from these developments, but it is certainly true that books like *The Prospect of Rhetoric: A Report of the National Development Project* (Bitzer and Black, eds. 1972) and articles like Robert L. Scott's "Rhetoric As Epistemic Ten Years Later" (*Central States Speech Journal,* 1976) were affecting influential thinkers in some composition programs in 1977.

Yet another school associated with "the new rhetoric" took the term literally. Chaïm Perelman and Lucie Olbrechts-Tyteca's *The New Rhetoric,* translated into English in 1969, gave a boost to people who wanted to organize their composition courses around argument. We have already noted that Richard Weaver's work in classical rhetoric di-

first fighting our way through Derrida's available work and then moving on to the sort of theory being published in journals such as *Diacritics* and *Boundary 2.* This was heady stuff to a refugee from New Criticism and current-traditional rhetoric.

I don't remember exactly how I made the connection between pre-classical rhetorical thought and post-structuralism. I do remember mentioning the connection to members of my reading group, none of whom had heard of Gorgias but all of whom wisely cautioned me against falling into ahistoricism. (In the piece I opined that Gorgias escaped the metaphysics of presence through the simple expedient of antedating its invention.) I think now that what I intuited in 1977 was that both bodies of thought are interested in the rhetoricity, the performativity, of language. As a result both critique an emphasis on referentiality that would tie language to things or ideas, require it to serve substance rather than situation, and hence subordinate rhetoric to philosophy, theology, and/or science (take your historical pick).

I decided to try out the connection at the Wyoming Conference in 1978. I remember being pretty scared when I walked onto the stage in that auditorium on the Wyoming campus. I had given only five or six professional papers prior to that occasion. And

rected him toward argument: he proposed a course in argument based on four main appeals—definition, similitude, consequence, and testimony. And we have implied that the work of Burke on identification and the Chicago critics' emphasis on Aristotle and on rhetorical stance moved thinking about composition in the direction of argument. Perelman and Olbrechts-Tyteca's monumental work took argument as the basis for a reconception of all discourse, retheorized "audience" in a way that was useful for practicing rhetoricians, invented a new rhetorical term—"presence"—to designate rhetorical effects that occupy the foreground of an audience's consciousness, and reemphasized the utility of epideictic rhetoric in contemporary culture. When Perelman's condensed version of his work was completed in 1977 as *The Realm of Rhetoric* (translated into English in 1982), the broad application from his theories to pedagogy was complete. About the same time, the philosopher Stephen Toulmin's work on argument, visible first in his *The Uses of Argument* (1964), was gaining adherents in aca-

there were a hundred or so people in the audience, all of whom looked smarter and more experienced than me. I read my paper, and a long silence ensued. Finally, someone asked what deconstruction or sophistry had to do with teaching composition. I was pretty much at a loss for an answer, but the questioner seemed satisfied by whatever I said. As the session was breaking up, a distinguished-looking gentleman who had been seated in the front row approached the stage and suggested we go for coffee. I consented, hoping that I might have a chance during the conversation to come up with some better answer than I had given to the only question posed after my talk. My companion gestured to another gentleman standing nearby. As we waited for the second man to join us, my companion admitted how he had long been interested in the Sophists and was, in fact, working on the notion of *kairos* as this had been put to use in an early Christian context. He then introduced himself to me as Jim Kinneavy, and he introduced his friend as Ed Corbett. I was thunderstruck. I had read Kinneavy's weighty and influential *Theory of Discourse* from cover to cover, of course, as had everyone else I knew who was interested in composition. Corbett was, famously, the author of *Classical Rhetoric for the Modern Student,* and was at that time the editor of *CCC* to boot.

Unfortunately I was so starstruck that I remember very little of our conversation over coffee. I do recall that Kinneavy, work-

demic and pedagogical circles, particularly through the advocacy of Charles Kneupper at the University of Texas at San Antonio; with Richard Riecke and Allan Janik, Toulmin was completing *An Introduction to Reasoning* (1979), a book that would soon be changing profoundly the way argument was taught.

Finally, "new rhetorics" in 1977 were emerging from developments in literary theory that we outlined earlier. Most of those theories would come to influence conduct in the composition classroom in the 1980s, but as we have already seen in the case of Wayne Booth, reader-oriented criticism was changing the way people conceived of communication so that the old static model of active writer/speaker and passive audience/listener was being undermined. Walter Ong's much cited "The Writer's Audience Is Always a Fiction" (1975) hastened the appropriation of reader-oriented approaches. The "philosophy" of E. D. Hirsch's *The Philosophy of Composition* (1977) was also grounded in the pragmatics of reader-oriented work: his recommendation that teachers should work to help students achieve "relative readability" in

ing from memory, gave me a long list of scholarly citations on the Sophists. I wrote them all down. And at the end of our visit, Corbett said "We need more articles in *CCC* that are theoretical and historical. Why don't you send this piece to me?" Just like that. (Of course it didn't happen "just like that"—I revised the piece twice before Professor Corbett deemed it suitable for publication, mainly inventing an answer to that question posed in Wyoming).

I don't know whether meetings like this happen in other branches of the humanities—does Peter Brooks take assistant professors out for coffee and gently tutor them about what they should read before they go public with their work? My students find it hard to believe this story—they say that "stars" of this stature would never speak to them about their work today, at CCCC or anywhere else. If that is so, I am saddened. Bryan Short, Jim Kinneavy, and Ed Corbett have all passed away now. This little exercise has affirmed for me the importance of collegiality and friendship to the quality of professional life, and has confirmed as well the consolation of memory.

their prose drew less from theory, however, than from reading research in psychology.

But reader-oriented theory was not the only theory that was influencing compositionists. For instance, in 1977 Sharon Crowley was already thinking presciently through the implications of deconstruction for composition. Her "Of Gorgias and Grammatology," first published in 1979 but originally delivered at the 1977 Wyoming Conference, pointed out how deconstruction undermined current-traditional notions attached to voice, presence, and univocal meaning. Moreover, the 1976 publication of Richard Ohmann's *English in America: A Radical View of the Profession* stirred ideological waters in composition through its critique of privileged class interests in English departments. Ohmann's book challenged the New Critical evasion of politics by arguing that the discipline's retreat into close reading ultimately insulated the profession and made it complicit with the military-industrial complex. The book invited scholars and teachers of writing to think about the larger cultural values informing the skills they chose to teach as part of a required undergraduate writing course; indeed, as English teachers were being implored to lead the nation out of a literacy crisis, Ohm-

Sidebar: Rhetoric in Wyoming, 1977

John Warnock

In 1977, the ground was stirring ever so slightly in the English Department at the University of Wyoming. I'd been Director of Freshman English for three years. The university's summer Wyoming Conference, started by my colleague Art Simpson in 1974, was becoming a watering hole for us in the not-yet field of rhetoric and composition across the country. We'd had that memorable Rhetoric Institute at the Science Camp in the Snowies, with E.D. Hirsch, Ross Winterowd, and Dick Young in attendance, among others. We were about to establish a writing center in the department and to offer the first summer institute of the Wyoming Writing Project for teachers in the schools. We had on the

ann asked them to consider the cultural and economic implications of literacy itself.

All these calls for new intellectual underpinnings for composition and rhetoric were reinforced by a call for a general professionalization of the field that, it was thought, would help ameliorate the literacy crisis of the time. Composition was part of general faculty development trends in higher education during the 1970s. If teachers could be trained better to teach composition (it had been pretty generally assumed that anyone with advanced preparation in literary study was prepared de facto to teach writing), if more research could be done on college composition (few journals then carried essays on composition, few university presses would consider a book related to composition, and few formal studies on composition were being conducted since graduate programs seldom offered research-oriented graduate work in composition studies), and if professional organizations could be developed to encourage research and its dissemination to teachers, then improved pedagogy and improved student writing would follow. Indeed, the push for professionalization on the part of many teachers of composition also reflected a desire to take advantage of a propitious historical moment. Walker Gibson, a respected scholar who had con-

books for our TAs a graduate course in "The Practical Teaching of Writing and Literature." I was in the middle of doing a survey of writing across the university—who did it, when, what kinds, and what importance "writing" was taken to have in different fields.

But if the ground was stirring, the curriculum sat there like a stone. First semester: read and write "expository essays." Second semester: introduce students to literature and write critical papers. Since faculty members as well as TAs taught composition at UW, I needed to know that none of the stirrings was going to make any difference in how the faculty taught these courses. It was a sociable department and faculty colleagues came to the Wyoming Conference in July to meet people and listen to the bluegrass, but no one, almost, came to enter the conversation about rhetoric and composition.

tributed to composition by means of textbooks and his book on style, *Tough, Sweet, and Stuffy,* suggested that the literacy crisis just might be the thing to finally improve the professional prestige and working conditions of compositionists:

> Obviously, we are all working under the constraints of the current public brouhaha about literacy, a new rage for testing, a return to the basics, and all the rest of it. Much that has been thought and said on these matters, before and after that infamous article in *Newsweek* a couple years ago, is simplistic nonsense. But there is an opportunity here, in the general political climate, to do something useful, to make the teaching of writing, both in school and college, a serious and respected activity. If, out of the current clamor, nothing more happens except that budgets for composition get a little looser and that directors of freshman writing programs feel a bit less forlorn, these results alone will be welcome progress. ("Writing Programs" 19)

Professional development both led to and was enabled by the growing influence of new organizations. The International Society for the History of Rhetoric was founded late in 1976 and held its first con-

Sidebar: Gathering Options for the Teaching of English: Freshman Composition

Jasper Neel

No one ever had an easier "first book" (insofar as an edited collection can be called a "book") than I had. In fall 1976, Liz Wooten [later Cowan] was leaving her position as Director of English Programs at MLA; she was on her way to an appointment at Texas A&M. In an almost exact opposite travel path, I was taking a leave of absence from Baylor (which is in Waco, about fifty miles from A&M) to go to New York and assume Liz's job. Though we did not know each other prior to this "exchange of positions," Liz

ference in Zurich in July, 1977 (Murphy 2); an American chapter of ISHR (i.e., the American Society for the History of Rhetoric: ASHR) developed later that year; the Rhetoric Society of America was founded in 1968 (and began to emerge as a major force in the mid-1970s: see D'Angelo, "Professing"); and the Association of Teachers of Technical Writing and the Council for Programs in Technical and Scientific Communication both started in 1973. All of these organizations in 1977 were encouraging dialogue, distributing news of professional interest, and sponsoring conferences. Corbett, Winterowd, Lauer, Young, and some others, for example, over dinner at the first RSA meetings were talking about the formation of a field of rhetoric within English studies (Lauer, "Getting"). CCCC and NCTE were already well established in 1977, of course, and attendance at their national meetings was increasing steadily; membership in CCCC, numbered at 300 in 1971, would climb to 1200 by 1979. The Wyoming Conference on Freshman and Sophomore English, which had begun as a local effort to increase articulation between the University of Wyoming and the state's community colleges, was now taking a decided turn toward rhetoric and composition, and was expanding to include more national issues and speakers. Experienced scholars at Wyoming had a chance to nurture beginners because the format not only included conference papers but also placed well-known experts—in 1977 James

and I always found it amusing that we had done our dissertations at the same university under the same dissertation director.

When I reflect on this transition, I remember two salient, exceedingly odd characteristics. First, at that time, anyone with a PhD in English from any accredited university in the land (Liz and I had gone to Tennessee) could claim to be a specialist in what was gradually becoming the field of "Rhet/Comp." Both Liz and I had done dissertations on Restoration British poetry. Neither of us had even so much as a single course in anything like rhetoric, composition theory, pedagogy, the teaching and/or learning of writing, literacy, or any of the other "fields" that now make up Rhet/Comp. Rhet/Comp was so infra dig that those who claimed it as a professional self-definition were regarded by most of their teachers and peers as objects of pity (if not outright scorn). By in large, success in college English departments was measured by the degree to which one did not have to teach composition courses.

Kinneavy and Robert Scholes were invited speakers—in dormitories and dining halls and thus into proximity with younger teachers and scholars (Tilly Warnock personal correspondence). (In the summer of 1976, John Warnock and Ross Winterowd put together an even more informal three-day summer institute-of-sorts on rhetoric that included Frank D'Angelo, Richard Young, Patricia Sullivan, Janice Lauer, George Yoos, E. D. Hirsch, and a couple of others and that met in a cabin near the University of Wyoming [D'Angelo, "Professing" 272; Ede 61].) A small Conference on Language and Style, organized by Donald McQuade and his colleagues at the CUNY Graduate Center, brought Richard Larson, Kenneth Bruffee, Sondra Perl, Sandra Schor, Judith Fishman, John Clifford, Mina Shaughnessy, and Janet Emig together with others for discussions of stylistics and the teaching of writing that were published in 1979 as *Linguistics, Stylistics, and the Teaching of Composition.* Erika Lindemann arranged a meeting at the University of South Carolina in the summer of 1977 to help college and secondary teachers integrate writing into their teaching; the five-week event gave David Bartholomae, James Raymond, Rick Coe, Susan Miller, and Joseph Comprone an opportunity to share ideas, for all of them taught together, though not all of them for the full five weeks (Ede 58).

Anyone who wanted to go to CCCC and do a paper could. By publishing a book with the phrase "Freshman Composition" in the title, the MLA was announcing publicly that the time had come for reimagining what composition might be. In large part, of course, this change of heart was driven by a dramatic drop in interest in literature courses and a huge media outcry that writing was being taught poorly in K-16. The MLA membership, however grudgingly, could easily see where the 1980s dollars might be made.

Second, by the time I got to New York, Liz had already done almost all of the hard work on the book. She had served for a number of years as Chair of the Communication Division at a community college, been active for years in both NCTE and CCCC, and also active in the College English Association. She knew, in a way that I certainly did not, which composition programs across the country were worth publicizing. In effect, by leaving me a nearly

And finally, important new journals began to emerge: *Freshman English News* (now *Composition Studies*) in 1972; *Teaching English in the Two-Year College* in 1974; the *Technical Writing Teacher* (now *Technical Communication Quarterly*) in 1974; the *Journal of Basic Writing* in 1975; and *The Writing Lab Newsletter* (edited by Muriel Harris), which first appeared in 1977–78. In 1976, reflecting the growing professional status accorded rhetoric and composition within the academy, the *Rhetoric Society of America Newsletter,* begun in 1970 by George Yoos, was given the more scholarly appellation *Rhetoric Society Quarterly.*

Even the Modern Language Association was beginning to get into the act. In 1975, a Division on the Teaching of Writing, with Edward Corbett as chair, was established within the organization. The following year, a meeting of composition directors was organized by Corbett, Harvey Wiener, and Kenneth Bruffee in order that directors might begin to share information and professionalize their positions. When the room for the meeting unexpectedly filled (December 26, 1976), the WPA—Writing Program Administration—was formed with Wiener as first President, to some extent in the spirit of the famous depression-era "other" WPA, and the entity known more and more as "the composition program" henceforth gained visibility, formality, and credibility (Wiener, personal interview). WPA and its new board of directors during 1977 initiated a program of sharing information (what

done project, she left me an education in how writing programs could (and did) operate effectively. All I had to do was encourage a few tardy authors, carry out some editorial polishing, and then see the book through publication. I suggested to Liz that we co-edit the book because she had already done so much. She responded that the book would never appear if I did not take it over and that another edited collection would be of little value to her, but, since I had none, of much value to me.

Thus, I was able to publish a collection focusing on a field in which I had great interest, but about which I knew nearly nothing. And when the book came out, *Viola!* I was a bona fide Rhet/Comp specialist. Now, of course, it would be "First-Year Writing." Then, no one noticed the word "freshman."

is now known as the journal *WPA* was then a newsletter, the first issue of which is dated March, 1977), preparing workshops for program administrators, and developing program evaluation teams.[36]

Beyond new organizations and journals, the impulse to professionalize manifested itself in increased attention to research in the teaching of writing. Because new composition courses and new students required more professional placement and evaluation methods, formal research into testing and evaluation that was especially interesting to administrators was also emerging: an example is Charles Cooper and Lee Odell's *Evaluating Writing,* published by NCTE in 1977. Perhaps in the spirit of Richard Ohmann, others began to explore the ideologies informing research into the writing process—for example, Richard Lloyd-Jones's "The Politics of Research into the Teaching of Composition" in the 1977 *CCC* and Robert VanDeWeghe's *ADE Bulletin* essay examining the place of research in establishing a disciplinary basis for composition.

All these attempts to professionalize through publication, organization, and research shook the foundations of writing programs across the country. In her study of 44 writing programs that appeared in the early 1980s, Carol Hartzog pinpointed 1977–1979 as the critical period of writing program development. Largely in response to the "neglect and disrespect" accorded to writing courses in the 1960s,

Sidebar: Rhetoric Seminar on Current Theories of Composition

Janice Lauer

In 1976, I initiated the first of thirteen two-week summer seminars at the University of Detroit. They were offered to meet the needs of teachers of composition, who had difficulty finding a point of entry into this emerging field and its expanding theory and research. I wanted the seminars to be credit-bearing graduate courses, offering three to four hours of credit (or official audit), requiring extensive reading, discussing, and writing in order to show that R/C theory was worthy of graduate study. Over the

Hartzog explained, universities were feeling pressure to prove the academic worth of their writing programs by the mid-seventies (6). In response to these pressures, the administration of composition programs and the theories that inform them became the subject of much discussion by mid-decade. Of particular note in this regard is Jasper Neel's *Options for the Teaching of English: Freshman Composition,* which was published by MLA in 1978. Neel's volume provides an overview of how composition programs in 18 colleges and universities of varying size and location were run during the mid-1970s. In his introduction, Neel identifies increased attention to the systematic administration of writing instruction as a distinguishing professional feature of the decade. Noteworthy also, according to Neel, was the new value being accorded to writing instruction, which "teachers and administrators have begun to see [. . .] as an end in itself, not a temporary assignment on the way to bigger and better things" (v). Reflecting this elevated status, universities now began hiring faculty specifically to coordinate composition programs. For example, Winifred Horner, Chairman of Lower Division Studies at the University of Missouri, Columbia in 1977, explained in Neel's book that the university's composition program was "coordinated by two regular faculty members hired for that purpose, one whose specialty is rhetoric and linguistics and the other whose specialty is Renaissance rhetoric" (Horner 58).

thirteen summers, the seminar actually became a record of an expanding discourse community whose resources grew remarkably. The seminar site showcased a lengthy bibliography of books and articles on rhetoric and composition theory as well as journals—all in a Resource Room for browsing.

The idea for a seminar format came to me from a summer Linguistics Institute at the University of Michigan that I had attended in the sixties. This traveling academy brought leading linguists to one place, enabling attendees to take courses from such scholars. I asked my friend Ross Winterowd to co-host the first seminar. Over the years, the seminar was a collaborative effort, co-taught each summer by around eight composition theorists whose work was contributing to the emergence of this field, including, in addition to Ross and me, Richard Young, Gordon Rohman, Gene Montague, Jim Berlin, Ed Corbett, Janet Emig, Linda Flower, James Kinneavy, Andrea Lunsford, Louis Milic, James Moffett,

This increased focus on the administration of composition programs nurtured another important force for professional development in composition and rhetoric—the expansion of discussion, both formal and informal, about the teaching of writing within composition programs. Regular staff and committee meetings (and the post-meeting conversations that inevitably followed) were regularizing teaching practices and expanding teachers' knowledge of developments in composition theory. What Donald McQuade, then Director of the Writing Program at Queens College, said of his program in 1977 was true of many: "To trace the development of the Writing Program at Queens College is to describe a gradual transformation from the privacy of personal practice to a collective enterprise that opened abundant prospects for intellectual and professional growth" ("Writing Program" 17).

Many English departments, often fitfully and in spite of themselves, coincidentally began to offer extensive teacher-training and graduate-level coursework—and then graduate degrees and emphases—in composition and rhetoric in order to develop a new generation of formally prepared teachers of composition. Young teachers who appreciated the prospect of a career in composition teaching, especially at a time when jobs in the traditional areas of English studies were in very short supply, were drawn to the courses. And the courses were

Frank O'Hare, Father Walter Ong, and Louise Phelps; and it was sustained by a hardworking talented staff of three or four graduate students each year.

Much to our surprise, sixty-two people attended that first seminar from 21 states, including Hawaii and Alaska. The seminar drew college writing instructors with PhDs in literature, community college instructors, high school teachers, and a few graduate students. The participants ultimately included 442 people from every state in the U.S.; Puerto Rico; the Canadian provinces of Alberta, British Columbia, Ontario, Nova Scotia, and Newfoundland; and England. In addition to writing instructors, the seminars enrolled psychologists, deans, chairs of departments, publishing representatives, curriculum supervisors, and professional writers in the workplace. All of these great people were willing to sacrifice time and money to study composition theory. During the two weeks, all of us benefited from lectures, spirited whole

needed. In his 1977 study of eighteen composition programs, Ross Winterowd found that at all but one of the PhD-granting institutions studied, more than 85 percent of the composition courses were taught by graduate students (v), usually graduate students in literary studies. Departments across the country therefore began to make concerted efforts to prepare graduate assistants in the theory and teaching of writing. Methods of teacher preparation and development, as identified in Neel's *Options for the Teaching of English: Freshman Composition,* included pre-semester training sessions, required courses on pedagogical methods, weekly or bi-weekly staff meetings, prescribed syllabi, regular workshops, and mentoring programs for new teaching assistants. Programs also made available professional resources, largely through textbook libraries and program handbooks. Beginning in 1974, for example, the University of Missouri required that new teaching assistants enroll in both practice-oriented workshops and a seminar entitled "Rhetorical and Linguistic Theory Applied to the Teaching of the English Language." Describing the course in 1977, Winifred Horner identified Corbett, Labov, Aristotle, Kinneavy, Toulmin, and Young, Becker, and Pike as central figures (61). At Ohio State, under the direction of Susan Miller, new teaching assistants were receiving one week of orientation as well as a "prescribed syllabus and a rhetoric and a reader selected by the director in consultation with the Freshman

and small-group discussions, lively evening parties, and weekend picnics and trips.

Even though the emphasis was on theory, not on Monday morning practices, participants testified in their evaluations that their new theoretical insights would inform their teaching. The seminar seemed to satisfy a hunger in the profession for rhetoric and composition theory, to hit a nerve among composition instructors, helping them to see writing as worthy of theory and research. Some said that the seminar opened up areas for their own scholarship and provided a composition community that they valued. I still treasure gifts given me at our farewell gatherings: tee shirts with titles like "Libation as Heuristic," "Rhetoric Spoken Here," "Chief Rhetor," and "Purdue Comp Camp"; a quill pen inscribed with "The Aristotelian Quill of Rhetoric"; a vase with the ashes of the *Harbrace Handbook*; a director's chair; and a bell to move us

English Policy Committee" ("Freshman English" 52). More important (since some form of orientation had been in place at OSU for years), the faculty at Ohio State voted in the spring of 1977 to begin requiring a one-quarter weekly workshop for new teachers and another elected course in rhetoric, composition, or language study to be taken during the first year of teaching ("Freshman English" 54–55). Similar programs emerged at the University of Iowa (under Cleo Martin), the University of Wyoming (under John Warnock), the University of Detroit (under Janice Lauer), and the University of Texas (under James Kinneavy).

More advanced and comprehensive graduate level coursework—and then graduate degrees and emphases—in composition and rhetoric were being developed as well in 1977. For instance, John Gage and Frank D'Angelo in 1977 were devising a sequence of four graduate seminars in rhetoric and composition at Arizona State University as a sort of minor within the standard fields of English and American literature (D'Angelo, "In Search of" 62). Ross Winterowd and his colleagues at the University of Southern California began a PhD program in 1973, and enrolled promising scholars such as Timothy Crusius and Tilly Eggers [later Warnock]. Texas Christian University began offering a PhD in the same year. But in general, mainstream universities still avoided rhetoric and composition as an intellectual and professional field of study, and one observer in 1978 complained that only three institutions were offering PhDs in rhetoric (Stewart, "Composition Textbooks" 176). Edward Corbett was editing *CCC* from Ohio State, but he was only beginning to offer graduate courses there, for example; and though he did direct Andrea Lunsford's dissertation on basic writing, that was one of only two dissertations produced at Ohio

from deafening informal discussions at breaks to formal sessions. I will be forever grateful I had the chance to meet and learn from so many colleagues dedicated to composition instruction and its guiding theories. I have described this seminar more fully in an essay, "Disciplinary Formation: The Rhetoric Seminar," in Ross Winterowd's festschrift in a 1998 issue of *JAC,* incorporating reactions from a number of participants.

State in the 1970s on a non-literary subject out of a total of over 125 (Strain 73). Miami University in 1977 required three courses in the "College Teaching of English" of all the students in its fledgling PhD program in English, including introductory survey courses in rhetoric and linguistics, but other advanced seminars in rhetoric and composition were still missing. Thus, what James Kinneavy had said in 1971, amid his own efforts to incorporate advanced study in composition and rhetoric into his department at the University of Texas–Austin (which he succeeded in creating through a PhD emphasis in 1979), was still generally true in 1977: "Composition is so clearly the stepchild of the English department that it is not a legitimate area of concern in graduate studies [nor yet] even recognized as a subdivision of the discipline of English" (*Theory* 1).

Composition and rhetoric were sometimes treated more hospitably in less conventional graduate programs. It was the University of Illinois–Chicago and Texas Woman's University[37] that made a space for advanced studies in rhetoric and composition during the 1970s, not Illinois at Urbana-Champaign or Texas–Austin; it was the University of Louisville that initiated a PhD in composition soon after Joseph Comprone arrived in 1976, not the University of Kentucky; it was Indiana University of Pennsylvania that offered doctoral study in composition, not Indiana University–Bloomington or Penn or Penn State; and it was North Carolina–Greensboro which acted in that state, not the flagship campus at Chapel Hill. Rensselaer Polytechnic Institute did not even have an English department, but it did offer a graduate program in communication and rhetoric (begun in the late 1960s), one which attracted Carolyn Miller as a student in 1976. Carnegie Mellon University, a 1968 amalgam of the Mellon Institute, Margaret Morrison College, and Carnegie Tech, developed its PhD when Richard Young arrived as Head in 1978 (Enos, email to Jack Selzer). Having evaluated the department as an outside consultant while he was at Michigan, Young moved quickly to hire new faculty (e.g., Richard Enos in 1979) and to get his new program in place. Meanwhile, Janice Lauer, a University of Michigan graduate who had worked with Richard Young on a dissertation evaluating invention heuristics, began a two-week, three-credit Summer Seminar in Rhetoric and Composition at the University of Detroit in 1976—an effort "to offer a sustained and coherent opportunity for people to read and discuss" composition theory and pedagogy (Lauer, "Constructing" 392). Then, after an outside review team that included Edward P. J. Corbett in 1978 noted that the English department at Purdue University could be strengthened by a graduate program in composition (Lauer, personal correspondence), Lauer went to Purdue in 1980 to continue her summer seminar (which persisted through the summer of 1988) and to develop a substantial graduate program. Carnegie Mellon and Purdue were by no means alone, of course: the 1994 *Rhetoric Review* survey of doctoral programs reveals that a great number of English departments stampeded to add doctoral study in rhetoric and composition in the four or five years after 1977.

Conclusion: Spreading the News

The new intellectual directions and schools of thought in the field in 1977 were tremendously stimulating, and they generated not only the passionate disciples and programs that we have named but also any number of inventive syntheses of them. Frank D'Angelo, for example, was resuscitating the modes with the help of various pieces of the new scholarship in his *Conceptual Theory of Rhetoric* (1975) and in his 1977 textbook *Process and Thought in Composition.* In one sense D'Angelo hearkened back to Bain in regarding the modes as having correspondences with the ways the brain operated. But D'Angelo's rhetoric was also an invigorating hybrid in that his sense of the way the brain operated was informed not by Bain's faculty psychology but by Gestalt and cognitive psychology and by structural linguistics. If he included "static logical topics" like description, narration, division, classification, and comparison, he also made room for "progressive" and "nonlogical" topics; he was attentive to the canons of invention and arrangement; and he somehow also synthesized into the 180 pages of *A Conceptual Theory* things as various as classical rhetoric, tagmemics, Burke's dramatism, structuralism, discourse analysis, process pedagogy, stylistics, and even citations that the expressivists would approve. Similarly, Ann Berthoff was beginning to synthesize into her years of practical experience as a writing teacher insights from I. A. Richards, Charles Sanders Peirce, Lev Vygotsky, and Paulo Freire, all of whom she would come to promote to great effect in her 1981 book *The Making of Meaning.*

The new directions and syntheses—and the general ferment developing around composition in 1977—were also apparent in three especially propitious scholarly efforts to develop and share new knowledge about rhetoric and composition. One example was Janice Lauer's summer seminar, which we have just commented on. The others were William Coles's NEH seminar on "Teaching Writing: Theories and Practices" and Richard Young's NEH seminar on "Rhetorical Invention and the Composing Process."

Coles first offered his seminar in the summer of 1977, and it continued to meet for the next three summers. Steeped in the educational and cultural troubles of the day, the seminar began with explorations of the literacy crisis. As Coles explained in his 1979 report to NEH, he encouraged participants to question the meanings of literacy and what might be meant, exactly, by the term "literacy crisis." Next Coles engaged participants in sustained conversations about the pedagogical implications of the literacy crisis and introduced the most important approaches being taken to the teaching of writing at the time: the "traditional approach (as represented by such writers as O. B. Hardison and Kierzek), the approach of the so-called 'new rhetoricians' (as represented by Winterowd and D'Angelo), the approach of writing as self-expression (Macrorie and Elbow), writing as style (Morse, Richard Lanham), writing as language-using (Coles, Gibson, and Roger Sale), and so forth" ("Letter to Dr. Dorothy Wartenberg" 3). Then he asked participants to contribute to larger professional conversations by preparing conference papers ("Letter to Dr. Dorothy Wartenberg" 3–4). Reflecting the growth and importance of community and two-year colleges, Coles decided in 1979 to restrict participation in his seminar to teachers from those institutions. In his report on that 1979 seminar, the first offered to teachers not working in four-year colleges and universities, Coles explains how he had come to realize the importance of the biases towards teachers in two-year and community college settings: "Though my experience with individual teachers from community colleges had been good in past summer seminars, [. . .] I wasn't sure about a seminar containing *only* such people. [. . .] Without realizing it, I was seeing teachers from two-year colleges in much the same way the academic community imagines the basic writer—rather like the inhabitants of the bar in *Star Wars*" ("Letter to Dr. Dorothy Wartenberg" 5). But after leading his first seminar exclusively for those teachers, Coles felt energized: "I feel that my work this year," he wrote, "may be the most important I have done for the NEH" ("Letter to Dr. Dorothy Wartenberg" 5).

Young's NEH seminar was proposed in 1976–77, offered in the summer at Michigan in 1978 and at Carnegie Mellon University in 1979 and 1980, and offered again—especially memorably—at Carnegie Mellon during the full 1978–1979 academic year. In many ways a short description of the seminar serves as a fitting summary to this section of our story, for the seminar focused not only on the composing process but also on just about every other intellectual development then in the air. Young's proposal summarized the three goals that he sought to accomplish: a greater "understanding of four modern methods of invention (classical invention, Burke's dramatistic method, Rohman's pre-writing, and Pike's tagmemic discovery procedure); an understanding of their historical and theoretical and practical contexts, including various conceptions of the composing process and their implications; and an ability to conduct significant independent research in the most important of the rhetorical arts" (qtd. in Almagno 48). The year-long seminar (the summer seminars were abbreviated versions), which began with lectures and intensive reading in the first semester and concluded with research presentations by participants in the second semester, raised the level of inquiry in composition studies and seeded the field with a corps of outstanding and ambitious beginning scholars. Indeed, a number of people whose work would be extremely important in the 1980s participated in the seminar and published the results of their inquiries, among them James Berlin, Lisa Ede, Charles Kneupper, Victoria Winkler [Mikelonis], Sam Watson, and Victor Vitanza. (Summer seminarians included Gene Garver, Charles Bazerman, Leslie Olsen, Carol Berkenkotter, and Gerald Mulderig.) At one point, Linda Flower and John Hayes interviewed the seminar participants (as "expert writers") for their own research into cognition, discovery, and the writing process that was eventually published as "The Cognition of Discovery" (1980). Other visitors to the seminar included Richard Ohmann, Janice Lauer, Alton Becker, and William Coles; and on one occasion the entire group drove to Penn State to meet with Henry Johnstone, editor of *Philosophy and Rhetoric* (Vitanza, "Retrospective"; Young, personal correspondence).

Victor Vitanza spoke for many when he commented on his own experience of the seminar: "I got more than I could ever dream of getting. This event made my professional life" (Almagno 50). In part that was because so many of the participants collaborated so freely, thus helping to mark collaboration as an accepted and natural part of professional behavior in the field. Vitanza, Watson, Ede, and Sharon Bassett, for instance, put together a presentation on "Evaluation and Tagmemics" for a 1979 conference; and James Berlin and Robert Inkster collaborated on "Current-Traditional Rhetoric: Paradigm and Practice" for *Freshman English News* (an article that offered a taxonomy of the field that Berlin would elaborate in *Rhetoric and Reality*). The project that was perhaps most closely associated with the NEH seminar was the journal *PRE/TEXT,* invented and edited by Vitanza, who invited all participants in the seminar to sit on the editorial board. The subject matter and editorial thrust of *PRE/TEXT* were intended to be "genuinely exploratory [and] tentative" by Vitanza, and an important objective of the journal was to displace negative connotations associated with rhetoric in the academy and to open up a dialogue for those interested in exploring new directions in rhetoric and composition (Almagno 62; Vitanza, ed.).

5 Composition in 1977: A Close Look at a Material Site

It is easier to understand how the strands of the national conversation about composition were being played out and easier to appreciate the material consequences of the national debates if they are examined in relation to a particular scene. It is also easier to understand how scholarly discussions about composition are constrained by local institutional conditions if one program is examined closely. Consequently, we examined in detail the discussions about composition that were taking place at Penn State's University Park campus against the backdrop of national developments. In part our decision was prompted by expedience—by our proximity to Penn State archives, secondary sources, and local personalities. However, we also had reason to believe—and our reasons were borne out by our research—that the discussions about composition at Penn State's University Park campus in 1977 did indeed mirror (and complicate) in elaborate, telling, and consequential ways the discussions that were taking place across the country about composition and did permit us to fill out our account of 1977 in ways that we could not have imagined beforehand. While Penn State's individual case is in some ways perhaps anomalous, it is in other ways highly instructive, for the general sense of crisis that animated the year 1977 as far as composition was concerned also animated the local situation—albeit with local twists. And an account of the efforts and counter-efforts of many parties at Penn State—faculty in English, faculty in other disciplines, administrators, members of the faculty senate—is instructive for indicating how responses to the crises in the university and the profession were being negotiated in 1977.

In the middle years of the 1970s, fissures had been developing in a successful system of writing instruction that had been in place for some years at Penn State. A switch from the tenure-line staff who had taught the first-year course and technical writing courses through the mid-1950s to the combination of tenure-line, graduate-student, and part-time faculty teachers who were staffing it twenty years later brought to the program unanticipated problems in curriculum and working conditions. Changes in institutional priorities also affected the conduct of composition in important ways. An expansion in student numbers and the presence of students who were perceived as ill-prepared for college writing created new needs that had to be addressed. Budgetary pressures created instructional stresses and constrained decision-making even as the new circumstances required new thinking and resources. And developments in composition scholarship nationwide were influencing, invigorating—and in some ways incapacitating—the whole enterprise.

Stormclouds

While the College of the Liberal Arts contemplated its future in that spring 1977 faculty conference that we described at the end of chapter two, Penn State was suffering through one of its worst budgetary crises ever. As we have already indicated, economic and political challenges in Pennsylvania were leading to unprecedented difficulties for public higher education in the state. When the state budget and consequently the delivery of the university's appropriation were delayed in 1977 by the legislature—the university was to have received approximately 35 percent of its funding from state appropriations (Oswald 205)—the absence of funds placed immense pressure on existing departments to cut back on expenditures.[38] Even without the delays, however, the budget for the university would have been inadequate. In February 1976, Penn State President John Oswald wrote to Henry Cianfrani, head of the Pennsylvania Senate Appropriations Committee, to request substantially greater funding because, he argued, "The proposed appropriation increase contained in the Governor's Budget for 1976–77 falls far short of meeting Penn State's basic needs. The recommended increase is about 29 percent of the amount needed" (Oswald 1). State appropriations had simply not kept up with the inflationary pressures that were standard during the 1970s. From 1971 to 1976, the Consumer Price Index rose from 123.1 to 158.6, a cumulative increase of 37 percent, but state appropriations per full-time student rose only from $1392 to $1687, a cumulative increase of just 22.1 percent. As a result, Penn State was forced to raise tuition significantly and to cut spending whenever possible, even on things considered essential. A May 12, 1975 memo on curricular reform in composition therefore devoted over a page to the "current paper shortage" which was discouraging teachers from reproducing student work for class discussion (Ebbitt, "Memo to Arthur O. Lewis").[39]

The university felt particularly strained by the increasing presence of non-traditional students who were seen as underprepared for Penn State coursework and who needed the support of new infrastructures. National and local concerns about remediation and basic skills increased the university's interest in professional development that would prepare faculty to meet the needs of these new students; the university also became interested in new curricular designs that would (it was hoped) enable these students to function successfully at Penn State. The pressures to prepare the university for new student populations were compounded by increasing complaints from the larger community that higher education was failing to equip students adequately with basic skills: the consensus was that Johnny and Janie couldn't write any better in Pennsylvania than they could elsewhere. In early 1977 the Joint Presidential-Senate Commission to Study Remedial Education conducted extensive research on the preparedness of incoming Penn State students in response to "assertions from both within and without the university community that numerous college graduates write badly or are unable to do basic mathematics" ("Legislative Report" iii). The Commission found that SAT-verbal scores for Penn State students had dropped from 520 to 470 between 1967 and 1976 (reflecting an expansion of the student body) and concluded that "deficiencies in some skills, notably writing, are so widespread that irrespective of future trends, a substantial attack on the problem must be made over the next several years" (1). In 1976, the Developmental Year Committee of the Faculty Senate also recommended that greater emphasis be placed on remedial education. A committee appointed to discover the extent of the problem concluded that 25 percent of incoming freshmen throughout the Penn State system were scoring "inadequately" in English in 1976; 46 percent of newly admitted students in 1975–76 took basic skills courses of one kind or another (Senate Special Committee on Basic Skills, "Legislative Report" n.p.). A Basic Skills Committee was consequently charged with studying and proposing "solutions to the need by many students for instruction which is preparatory to college-level courses in areas of quantitative and qualitative thought and articulation" (Senate Special Committee on Basic Skills, "Legislative Report" n.p.) In proposing "basic skills" programs at Penn State, the Committee was clearly responding to larger social issues that involved far more than students' inability to write grammatically correct sentences. The Committee stressed the "necessity" of adding basic skills courses in the face of a "dizzying list" of possible "causes" for the decline in students' skills—"television, permissiveness, the telephone, drugs, 'creative writing' [in high schools], mass education, Vietnam, poor teaching in the schools, popular writers, or computers" ("Legislative Report" 1). The concerns expressed by the Committee were already influencing great changes within the Penn State English department.

A Department in Trouble

As Penn State and its College of the Liberal Arts struggled with financial difficulties and with the challenge of underprepared students, so did the English department at University Park. Drastic changes in enrollment patterns, including a dramatic plunge in undergraduate majors in English that was in keeping with the national trends we surveyed earlier and that poisoned the professional atmosphere in the department, marked the 1976–77 academic year. John Moore, then an assistant professor of English specializing in the poetry of Edmund Spenser, recalls the drop in majors during the 1970s in a simple sentence: "The bottom just fell out" (personal interview). In 1969–70, the English department counted 520 majors, according to a 1974 self-assessment; by 1977, the number had dwindled to just 236 (O'Donnell). Total enrollment in upper-division creative writing and literature courses fell from 3,836 in 1972–73 to about 2,300 in 1977–78; in 1969–70, the department ran about 75 sections of upper-division courses, but in 1976–77, the number was about half that.

The graduate program in English was in similarly dire straits in terms of student numbers. In concert with national trends, the number of graduate applications had dropped 30 percent, from 176 to 123, in just one year (1976 to 1977)—but that decrease was only the latest one: from the 1969–70 academic year to the 1976–77 year, applications for graduate study in English dropped an astounding 78 percent, from 559 to 123 (Liberal Arts Steering Committee 40). A consequent steep reduction in the size of the graduate program required the cancellation of many sections of traditional graduate offerings in literary study and left many tenured faculty with precious little to teach. Many of the graduate students admitted (nearly all of them teaching composition under assistantships) were less capable than the graduate students admitted just a few years before. Indeed, the department was unable to fill all of its teaching assistantships with qualified applicants, and began to offer a few of its lines to graduate students in other departments—some of whom found themselves teaching composition as well. Meanwhile, more "practical" departments in the College of the Liberal Arts were gaining majors and students—Public Administration and Journalism majors rose by 279 percent and 138 percent respectively—and many students were running away from the Liberal Arts completely, especially to the College of Agriculture and the College of Health and Physical Education, which both doubled their relative percentage of university enrollment (Coelen 41).[40]

The department was less able to face its difficulties than it might have been because of leadership problems. In 1973, the legendary and long-term department Head, Henry Sams, had retired. Sams, who had come to Penn State from the University of Chicago in 1959 with a mandate to build an English department in the image of those at other research universities, had steered it through heady times in the direction of literary study (as was conventional in the 1950s and 1960s, rhetoric at Penn State was relegated to strong departments of Philosophy and Speech Communication, which had together sponsored *Philosophy and Rhetoric* since 1968 without much notice in English); and he was able to hold its various factions together during the well funded 1960s by the force of his vision, personality, and competence. But Sams was succeeded by one head who was ousted late in 1974 after over a year of debilitating divisiveness concerning a whole host of issues, and then by a temporary head (Associate Dean Arthur Lewis, who necessarily kept to a holding action for the remainder of the 1974–75 school year). In the fall of 1975 Robert Worth Frank, a respected medievalist, assumed the headship and served until his own retirement in 1979. In retrospect, it seems apparent that anyone would have had trouble succeeding as a department leader in the direct wake of Henry Sams and in the social circumstances of the time; but in any event the various administrative upheavals—five heads in less than a decade, counting Wendell Harris, who arrived in 1979—did make it difficult for faculty to address enrollment shifts, professional controversies, and intellectual developments within the field.

Perhaps most important, because the literature and creative writing courses that most English faculty had grown so accustomed to teaching were now much scarcer, composition, technical writing, and business writing suddenly became the only growing enterprises, and closer to the center of the department's activities. While total enrollments in undergraduate literature courses were plunging, composition enrollments remained extremely healthy, and interest in business writing and technical writing increased substantially—from 1,196 students in 1972–73 to 2,835 in 1977–78. "A lot of faculty returned to teaching comp in the early and mid 1970s," recalls John Moore. "The composition program obviously became the object of a lot of scrutiny because suddenly [. . .] we were all teaching it" (personal interview). "A lot of scrutiny" is putting it mildly. Many faculty resented the new prominence afforded to writing courses in the face of the lack of literature majors and students, resisted the new attention given to the enterprise (not to mention a proposed mandate offered by the departmental administration that all tenure-line faculty teach at least one composition course), and took out their professional frustrations on it. A number of faculty even blamed composition for the drop-off in enrollments, offering one or another prescription for making composition a more attractive introduction to English studies. Harvey Wiener, Director of Basic Writing at Penn State in 1976–77, twenty years later remembered well the hostility created by this shift of focus from literature to composition: "Things were very precarious at Penn State at that time in terms of the role of composition in the department. I think there was a lot of hostility toward the influence of the writing courses" (personal interview).

Trouble in Composition

Indeed, there were good reasons for some of the hostility, for during the early to middle 1970s composition at Penn State was showing tangible signs of a substantial deterioration in quality. Course texts, writing assignments, and even essential course goals had proliferated willy-nilly in the wake of the loose administrative structure of the freshman writing program that had served well enough during the 1950s and early 1960s, when most instructors were tenure-line faculty, but that ill suited the new conditions of the 1970s.

Until about 1960, composition at Penn State had been taught by a largely tenure-line faculty of the Department of English Composition that was made up of writers of various kinds (including, at one time or another, the novelists John Barth and Joseph Heller, the poet Theodore Roethke, and former professional technical writers such as Kenneth Houp, William Damerst, and Robert Weaver). That large Department of English Composition operated even as a parallel Department of English Literature, composed of about a dozen faculty, handled the literary part of English studies. In 1957, the university combined the departments in the wake of an external evaluation—it was a kind of "shotgun marriage," remembers Robert Frank, who arrived in 1958 (personal interview)—but the two factions coexisted fairly peacefully during the 1960s: literature courses were taught by an increasing faculty of English PhDs, while composition and the writing major remained the domain of a strong if dwindling corps of writers, supplemented gradually by some of the PhDs and MAs in English literature. The annual Penn State catalog that listed all faculty in English described them as professors "of English" or "of English Composition" depending on their origin and responsibilities. But as enrollments at Penn State increased, as the university pursued more of a research profile that emphasized faculty with doctorates, and as graduate studies in the English department consequently grew more important (and in keeping with most American universities, graduate studies in English meant literary study, not composition or creative writing), the formal designation "of composition" was phased out for English faculty, and composition instruction was gradually turned over to teaching assistants pursuing literary degrees. As their numbers increased, supervision of the two required freshman courses, English 1 and English 3 (the first a course organized around the modes of exposition, the second a course in literary analysis that we will discuss in a moment), became more of a challenge—and more of an unmet challenge.

In the 1960s and 1970s, the subject matter and course objectives for both English 1 and 3 originated in committee-established reading lists from which individual instructors could select course material. Each writing course had a "course chairman"—there was no Director of Composition—who supervised the committee text-selection procedure. The 1969 "Policy Governing the Freshman Writing Program" elaborated on this committee process:

> The course chairman will conduct meetings of the course staff, the committee of the whole, to review course objectives, standards, and the selection of texts.

> [. . .] As this committee of the whole [. . .] selects texts for the coming year, it will make a list large enough to permit choice within itself, in a ratio of 1 to 2—that is, a fixed list to be used by those who may not exercise choice [i.e., graduate students new to the course], and a larger list from which those who may exercise choice may select.

Despite this on-paper procedure, there developed over time no standardized criteria for selecting works to include on the lists. According to Ron Maxwell, then an assistant professor in the department, the composition program "was a leaderless group of chairmen and we did a lot of squabbling. The courses [i.e., English 1 and 3 from year to year] were [. . .] as different as the individuals who chaired them" (personal interview). Once a committee did come up with an "official" list of textbooks, little was done to enforce adherence to the lists or to the assumptions implied by the lists. According to Judd Arnold, a member of the Renaissance faculty at the time, "The composition program was weakly led by caretakers like me. [. . .] We were simply trying to hang on to a structure that had been given to us. [The program] for about three or four years had no significant leadership. [. . .] Faculty [in the early 1970s] were not really supervised in these matters" (personal interview). Nor were teaching assistants. As Robert Frank recalls, it was simply assumed in the profession that "anyone could teach composition" without special preparation or standard syllabi, and the assumption carried over to young teaching assistants, who were taking over more and more sections of composition (personal interview).

The lack of standardization and preparation were particularly obvious in English 3, the second required course in the first-year sequence. Although readings varied among the various sections of English 1, English 1 assignments usually focused on the so-called "expository modes" that were the stuff of most composition textbooks of the period—description, narration, comparison, analysis, and so forth—and so consistency from section to section was fairly stable. The syllabus emphasized correctness and standard organizational patterns, proclaiming that English "concerns itself primarily with the acquisition of skills [and] rests on the assumption that the ability to write is best developed by organic stages: the less complex before the more complex, the smaller before the larger." (Freshman English Committee, *English 1* n.p.). English 3, however, was a site of far greater conflict and variation among instructors. Jeanne Fahnestock, a lecturer-rank instructor of the course in the early 1970s who is now teaching rhetoric and composition at the University of Maryland, recalls that English 3 "was a free-for-all. When I first started teaching as a part-timer, they really didn't give a darn what I taught. They hired me because I was a lit PhD, and they let me just make lit assignments and we were supposed to write papers somewhere in there" (personal interview). Nancy Lowe, another lecturer at the time, also remembers English 3 as a "kind of a free-for-all" in terms of what was actually taught in the course: "there were some courses written up [as examples], but there was nothing that said we had to do that. And so we had people teaching their dissertations" (personal interview). Ron Maxwell recounts the experience of a new teacher in the program in a similar fashion: "In retrospect [. . .] we were roughly handed a syllabus and told 'Good Luck.' We did have staff meetings and a little orientation [. . .] but nothing disciplined and thoughtful" (personal interview). Beginning teaching assistants were assigned in small groups of three or four to experienced faculty members, each of whom passed on his or her own wisdom—in small or large doses, depending on the faculty member involved—without much regard for the practices of others (Frank, personal interview).

Pedagogical approaches to the assigned texts seemed equally haphazard. A May 12, 1975 report on the situation concluded that "English 3 is not one course but many, many courses, some radically different from others" (Ebbitt, "Letter to Arthur O. Lewis"). Many teachers of English 3 approached it as a course in the Great Ideas of Literature, in part because the origins of the course encouraged them to do so. S. Leonard Rubinstein, the main engineer of English 3, described in the mid-1960s what he hoped the course could do. In articles in *College English* ("Composition: A Collision") and in Penn State's *Faculty Bulletin,* he described English 3 as a sequence of exercises in exposition grounded in the discussion of documents such as Hemingway's "A Clean, Well Lighted Place," Gertrude Stein's "Melanctha," Plato's *Apology,* and Dostoevsky's "The Grand Inquisitor." (One actual syllabus that we examined took students consecutively through poetry by Frost, Dickinson, Housman, Shakespeare, and Eliot; fiction by Hemingway, Crane, Roth, and Hawthorne; Albee's plays *The Zoo Story* and *The American Dream;* and Ellison's novel *Invisible Man.* Four short essays were assigned, two of them in-class themes, and there was a research paper.) Instructors were encouraged by Rubinstein's own textbook, *Writing: A Habit of Mind,* to fill the class by asking questions that would engage students in discussions that would subsequently lead to individual interpretations committed to paper; along the way, students would learn the rules for evidence and methods for clarifying and polishing academic arguments. Writing instruction was indirect and based "on the contention that a student eager to clarify his ideas about an exciting work is willing to learn what is necessary to make his ideas clear, strong, and valid" (Rubinstein, "New Approaches" n.p.).

A product of formalist criticism, the course had broad appeal, and it was successful indeed when instructors as gifted as Rubinstein himself taught it. (Robert Frank is not the only Penn Stater who recalls Rubinstein as "a tremendous teacher" [personal interview]. Frank's own daughter had taken composition from Rubinstein and found him to be "marvelous," and even now, years after his retirement, Rubinstein is regarded in the community as a memorable and charismatic teacher—if also as a bit of a curmudgeon.) Ron Maxwell has confirmed that Rubinstein's model from English 3 was pervasive in the department, that in the late 1960s and early 1970s "the aim in [English 3] was to [. . .] bring together a group of readings that spoke to each other, and then read them sequentially and encourage students to write in response to them, expecting that the early readings would have some relevance for later readings. [. . .] Folks liked teaching composition from readings. [. . .] We didn't have a notion that rhetoric was a discipline in itself" (personal interview). Edgar Knapp, then associate professor of English and education, confirms that in English 3 "literature [wa]s the center of it [. . .] where the ideas of [. . .] something like Machiavelli's *The Prince* would stimulate and would be the substance of composition" (personal interview). Making literature the focus of the course permitted literary scholars to promote and capitalize on their areas of interest. As Sharon Crowley has noted, "the practice of using literary texts in the required composition course carries enormous weight in the politics of English departments. [. . .] The presence of literature in that course affirms the status of literary studies as the defining activity of English studies" (*Composition* 87). The literature included within the composition courses at Penn State performed such an affirmation, without question. The devotion to literary study kept to a minimum attention to composition and rhetoric.

While Rubinstein himself was careful to warn that his course was "imperiled by the teacher who forgets the difference between the use of literary material for literary purposes and the use of literary material for compositional purposes" ("Composition: A Collision" 273), and while Judd Arnold and some others understood that in the course "you approached literary texts not to discuss the great ideas it might contain, but as bodies of evidence from which you could draw inferences, about which you could form judgments" (personal interview), as time went on and especially as new and inexperienced teachers began to dominate the staff, many teachers ignored those caveats. By the early 1970s there were a great many variations on Rubinstein's theme, especially since graduate student instructors were offered little supervision. By the end of the 1974–75 academic year, there were English 3 courses that "might better be labeled 'Introduction to Literature'"; courses based on themes; courses explicitly claiming to be "creative writing, encouraging, above all, expressiveness"; "four or five [courses] that seemed to be solid courses in the writing of expository and argumentative prose"; and several sections operating on an ad hoc basis, where "teachers improvise[d] from week to week" (Ebbitt, "Memo to Arthur O. Lewis").

Figure 1. Samuel Leonard Rubinstein. © Department of English, The Pennsylvania State University. Used by permission.

Figure 2. Wilma Ebbitt. © Department of English, The Pennsylvania State University. Used by permission.

Figure 3. Robert Frank. © Department of English, The Pennsylvania State University. Used by permission.

Moreover, some people were coming to question Rubinstein's literature-reverent approach to teaching writing. For some, the readings in a writing course came to function not as sources for Great Ideas or topics for papers, but as places to examine "essential questions" about the writing process, questions such as, "What is the writer's intention? What elements in the rhetorical situation help or hinder him [sic] in carrying out his intention? What choices does he make in developing, organizing, and presenting his ideas? Why *this* sentence pattern, *this* word—even *this* way of punctuating?" (Freshman English Committee, *English 3 Sourcebook* 3). According to this view, readings were supposed not only to generate ideas for writing but to serve primarily as sources for thinking about writing strategies and rhetorical choices. But even within this more student-writing-centered approach to English 3, pedagogical methods varied widely. According to Maxwell, there were at least two distinct ideas in the department about how writing should be taught: "There was a group in the department [. . .] which strongly believed you developed the ability to write with bricks and you accumulated those bricks with skills like grammar" (personal interview). Such an approach was consistent with the current-traditional textbooks that we mentioned in chapter four, ones beginning with words and then moving to sentences, paragraphs, and longer pieces of discourse. Maxwell adds, "Then there was another group of people who w[ere] very romantic [. . .] by distinction from this rather mechanical, rule driven process of teaching writing" (personal interview). These latter teachers' classroom practices, according to Maxwell, often developed out of the work of Ken Macrorie and other expressivists whose student-centered pedagogies developed out of the political values and educational reform movements of the 1960s.

Accompanying these questions about appropriate course content and pedagogical method, as we have already hinted, were concerns about the professional competence of freshman English instructors. In the spirit of faculty development then flourishing in higher education, Liberal Arts Dean Stanley Paulson urged the department to better prepare and professionalize instructors, especially graduate students. According to John Moore, who was a member of the Freshman English Committee in 1974–75, Dean Paulson had "got wind of some crisis. [. . .] The incompetence of the people teaching freshman English was suddenly brought to [his] attention, and he said, 'We need a new comp program'" (personal interview). The question of professional development for the composition staff had been simmering in the department since the gradual switch after the mid-1950s from freshman instruction exclusively by tenure-line faculty to instruction by a mixture of tenure-line and part-time faculty and graduate students thereafter—with the percentage handled by graduate students creeping up yearly. Without a well-developed system of accountability in place, without an orientation program for new teachers, and with course syllabi offering only the superficial guidance that one associates with an experienced faculty, instruction by graduate students was becoming uneven at best. During the early 1970s, Moore explains, "graduate students weren't trained to teach—no meetings, nothing like that" (personal interview). Marie Secor paints an even less appealing picture of the professional preparation of graduate students, whom she describes as "operating at varying degrees of irresponsibility" because of the lack of direction in the program (personal interview).

Deep mistrust of graduate-student instructors also resulted from graduate-student involvement in the campus protests of the late 1960s and early 1970s. In April of 1970, the campus branch of Students for a Democratic Society had protested military-supported research on campus and demanded, among other things, open enrollment policies (like the ones that would soon be in place at CUNY) for all who wished to attend Penn State. The SDS led a march followed by a sit-in at Old Main, the central administrative building that houses the university president's office. The demonstration turned confrontational, resulting in injuries to eighteen state troopers and the arrest of twenty-nine student protesters. Students harshly criticized the treatment of the arrested protesters at the hands of the state troopers and university representatives. In support of the arrested students, numerous faculty, staff, and instructors formed the University Strike Committee and threatened to shut down campus operations if the twenty-nine were not granted legal immunity. The spokesman for the Strike Committee, and one of the twenty-nine arrested at Old Main, was English graduate student Geoffrey Sills. Amid protests from several faculty members and graduate students in the department, Sills was dismissed from the university as a result of these activities.

Dissatisfaction with the conduct, purpose, and place of writing courses in the department in 1977 derived from other sources as well. The most vocal source were the personalities who taught courses for the department's Writing Option. As we mentioned, before 1957 faculty in English Composition at Penn State made up their own department, and they continued to offer their own major in writing even after they merged with the Department of English Literature; in 1977, therefore, an undergraduate majoring in English could still select either the Language and Literature Option or the Writing Option, both of which existed side by side under the rubric of "English" and each of which was supervised by a committee and program director. The Writing Option combined requirements in literature with courses in journalism, technical writing, fiction, poetry, nonfiction, and biography; it sought to prepare students for writing careers of many types, and its proponents averred that students in the Writing Option became versatile, well-educated, and well-rounded writers, not just narrowly prepared creative writers. Indeed, Writing Option faculty tended to disdain use of the term "creative writing," instead claiming that their goal was to prepare *writers* of various kinds—even as their relative numbers steadily declined in the department. Like many literature faculty in the mid-1970s, instructors and professors in the Writing Option were concerned about the quality of composition courses; some felt somewhat threatened by the growing prominence of composition courses that they could not effectively control (especially when they had strong professional reasons for what they thought composition courses ought to do), and several—notably Leonard Rubinstein but others as well—sought to maintain supervision over the courses themselves. Both literature and writing faculty, then, felt that they should have greater influence on the freshman composition courses in order to attract potential students for their program major option, and both camps were, with reason, suspicious of each other.

In 1976, consequently, in response to the growing dissatisfaction with freshman composition and to their own sense of marginalization within the English department, six English professors associated with the Writing Option offered their own plan for improving student writing. In their plan, the six pointed to the inadequacy of the existing courses. "Many [students] leave the university with degrees but without the reading, writing, and speaking skills to give their best in their post-college lives," they charged in an interview with a local newspaper. "At the same time," they continued, "the departments within the college which offer instruction in these skills often offer courses which overlap badly, or are focused too narrowly—or in any case do not seem to work" (qtd. In DuBois, 19). The professors' plan involved removing responsibility for teaching composition from the English department and its graduate students and locating it instead in a proposed new "School of Communications and Journalism" (DuBois) that would rely on tenure-line faculty with real-world experience in writing of one kind or another—in other words, in an academic unit that would re-establish the old Department of English Composition. In their plan to improve writing skills and writing instruction, the six professors, one of them former Writing Option Director Leonard Rubinstein, offered a particularly scathing critique of the graduate-student presence in the composition classroom: "We must stop using graduate students who, whatever their knowledge of literature, are themselves subliterate because they have never had a writing course above the freshman level" (qtd. in DuBois). Under the proposal, which also included provisions for creating new creative writing majors and minors, composition was to be taught strictly by professional writers.[41]

Concern about English 1 and 3 also came from faculty in other disciplines, some of whom felt, in an atmosphere of "back to basics," that the English department's composition courses were not accomplishing what they ought to in order to prepare students for other studies in the academy and for careers after graduation. In November 1976, Professor Eugene Goodwin, a former director of the School of Journalism at Penn State, said he had "observed students being turned away from the journalism program with Ds and Fs in their initial classes after getting As in freshman English" (qtd. in DuBois 19). Ron Maxwell recalls the sudden urgency for accountability; "I remember at some time in this era, the [faculty] senate did ask the English department who they thought they were by teaching these courses the way they did" (personal interview).

In response to some of the criticisms about the structure, purpose, and professionalism of the department in the mid-1970s and as part of its own internal reform efforts that we will turn to in a moment (for the department was not unaware of the problems), outside evaluators Erika Lindemann (then of the University of South Carolina) and Gary Tate (of Texas Christian University) were asked to conduct a joint evaluation of the program in the fall of 1977. In their report to Dean Paulson, Lindemann and Tate emphasized the conflicting approaches to teaching the freshman courses that prevailed at the time: "The courses seem to be transitional, moving away from past emphases on literature as a vehicle for writing to courses which focus more attention on the process students engage in as they write" (1). The report went on to note the "tension between the study of forms and study of process" in the syllabi observed and attributed this tension to an "inevitable heritage of previous syllabi which emphasized the written product rather than the composing process" (1). The process movement, as we shall see, was starting to make its mark, yet mainly the department was still judged, and judged harshly, by the quality of its students' products. Lindemann and Tate's report suggested that the department was "under unreasonable pressure to generate statistical data concerning the progress" (4) of students in the freshman writing courses—a clear attempt to respond to campus-wide calls for product-oriented assessment.

This concern for rigorous assessment and quantifiable results came to a head in the mid-1970s when the department's first official Composition Director, James Holahan (affiliated with the Writing Option and appointed for a short time, as we shall see, to bring order back to the English 1–3 sequence), introduced into English 1 the Minimal Essentials Test. In order to pass English 1, students had to achieve a minimum score on this exam on the conventions of Standard English: "grammar and diction," "punctuation," and "paragraphing." Students were given the test halfway through the course, and students who failed (i.e., got fewer than 60 percent of the questions correct) were offered the possibility of two retakes. Maxwell has called this test "the last straw" because "people who wanted [. . .] to teach writing in a more organized way than in a mechanistic way just were denied it" (personal interview). The exam led to protests of one kind or another from various composition instructors, both faculty and graduate assistants. Several graduate-student instructors—calling themselves the MLA / MET Liberation Army—circulated a biting parodic memo in July of 1974 that ridiculed the practices and goals of the Minimum Essentials Test. (Needless to say, the student essays from this period that we located have red-penned teacher comments that are focused almost solely on errors. And notes taken by student Thomas Bayer are full of tips such as "limit sentences to fewer than seventeen words," details on syntax and vocabulary, and diagrams of the five-paragraph theme, complete with "funnel" introduction and reverse-funnel conclusion.)

Attempts to alter curricula in response to changing economic and academic environments were also complicated for University Park faculty and curriculum planners by an inevitable and increasing tension between the sprawling, comprehensive University Park campus and the eighteen much smaller two-year campuses located around Pennsylvania (the Commonwealth Campuses) that offered associate degree programs as well as transfers to University Park baccalaureate programs. The tense economic times were especially pressing for Commonwealth Campus faculty, whose teaching assignments were heavier, who were usually less prominent professionally, and who enjoyed somewhat less job security than their colleagues at University Park. In response to their local concerns, the faculty and staff of the Commonwealth Campuses attempted in 1971 to unionize separately from the University Park campus, a move that was ultimately stymied by University Park administration.[42] Exacerbating the animosity generated by financial crises was a substantial difference in preparation between the student populations that Commonwealth Campus faculty faced and those encountered at University Park, where curricula were designed. On paper, English faculty members in all locations were part of the same department, but University Park committees in fact controlled curricula and policies. To the extent that Commonwealth Campus faculty felt that the curricula for English 1 and 3 were inappropriate for their students and circumstances, they went their own way and taught the courses as they saw fit. Several campuses, for example, balked at the idea of an exit exam for composition courses, arguing that it would mean greater work for those campuses than for University Park, which tended to get better prepared students.[43] Others devised more or less standard syllabi that they felt were appropriate for typical students on the Commonwealth Campuses (Frank, personal interview).

Financial and curricular difficulties on the Commonwealth Campuses and at University Park were accompanied by a general worry about the decline in quality of high school education in general and about the importance placed on reading and writing in particular. One faculty member, Martha Kolln, then Director of Basic Writing, explained early in 1978 to the *Harrisburg Evening News* that "college freshmen no longer have a history of reading and writing behind them. [. . . T]elevision has become a leisure time substitute for books" (qtd. in "PSU Teaching"). Television was not the only thing threatening the writing abilities of future college students. There was a sense that

Pennsylvania public high schools were failing their students. As one student complained to the *Harrisburg Evening News,* the loose elective system in Pennsylvania high schools put too much responsibility on irresponsible teens: "In ninth, tenth, and eleventh grades you're still too young to make these choices. [. . .] The students will go for the easy course every time" (qtd. in "PSU Teaching"). Reflecting these concerns, Kolln asserted that "These students grew up in the 1960s when education meant 'doing your own thing'" (qtd. in "PSU Teaching") rather than learning basic skills. Lindemann and Tate's report expressed similar disillusionment with public education at the time, suggesting that the basic writing program at Penn State would take time to be effective because "[t]welve years of public education cannot be undone overnight" (4).

6 Responding to the Crisis: Conversing about Composition at Penn State in 1977

Amidst concerns about how to respond to increasing numbers of underprepared students, a statewide and university budgetary crisis, local visions of intellectual chaos and aimlessness in the humanities, and difficulties in English studies and in its composition program, it is not surprising that the University Park English Department, under the leadership of Robert Frank, shifted into something of a crisis mode. For the department to respond adequately to the changing student populations faced both at University Park and the Commonwealth Campuses and to assert persuasively the importance of its freshman writing program, it needed to "retrain" its teachers and devise a "newer approach" to freshman composition (Lindemann and Tate). In other words, the problems that we detailed in chapters two and three as characteristic across the nation were indeed in evidence at Penn State, and faculty and administrators there looked to many of the same proposed solutions that we sketched in chapter four. In 1977, that meant considerable tension, as the means of retraining and the content of Penn State's "newer approach" were rapidly evolving and hotly debated.

Improving the Required Courses

Professor Wilma Ebbitt was named Composition Director in the early spring of 1975 and put in charge of revising the curriculum and improving instruction. Born in 1918 in the hamlet of Mossbank, Saskachewan, near Moose Jaw, and a Brown University PhD (1943), Ebbitt had come to Penn State in the fall of 1974 as a full professor after twenty-three years in the undergraduate college at the University of Chicago and recent visiting positions at the University of Colorado and the University of Texas at Austin. As we mentioned in chapter four, from 1945 until 1968 she had been a close colleague of Richard Weaver, Henry Sams, James Sledd, and any number of well known others associated with Chicago. There she had been heavily involved in the undergraduate writing program, won the Quantrill Award for Excellence in Undergraduate Teaching, supervised as its chair some of the famous staff meetings of the College English Committee, and sat in on a 1950 seminar that was led by Kenneth Burke and that included Sams and Sledd (Sledd, personal interview). Ebbitt (as well as Weaver and Sams) was among those present at the first meeting of the Conference on College Composition and Communication in 1949 (*Report of the Conference* 102). Though Ebbitt's dissertation had been on Margaret Fuller, most of her publications concerned composition in some way. Before coming to Penn State, she had coedited or cowritten several writing textbooks, including the widely adopted *Structure in Reading and Writing* (Scott, Foresman, 1961); *The Writer's Reader* (1968); and the *Writer's Guide and Index to English,* a pioneering textbook which had been started by Porter Perrin in the 1940s and which Ebbitt had joined for the influential fourth edition (1965) and took over completely for the fifth (1972).[44] With James Sledd, she put together *Dictionaries and THAT Dictionary* (1962), a casebook on a controversy over *Webster's Third International Dictionary* that was influenced by the new linguistics and intended to educate people about the nature of language variation and change.

Although she also retained a special interest in the literature of the American Renaissance, Ebbitt was brought to Penn State in large part because academic leaders realized that she might be very helpful in straightening out problems associated with composition (Frank, personal interview). And indeed she quickly, in her very first year, became heavily involved in the composition program. As Marie Secor noted, "Wilma Ebbitt came to Penn State with great intellectual seriousness about the teaching of writing, and she carried that respect for the enterprise into every aspect of her teaching, her professional life, and her influence on [the program]" (qtd. in "Ebbitt Fellowship"). Ebbitt's commitment to rhetorical education and her long-standing belief in the pedagogical seriousness required to teach composition were not universally welcomed by department members who were used to teaching composition in their own way (and who were not used to official guidelines and uniform standards). Writing Option faculty in particular wondered about the qualifications of a literature specialist in charge of a writing program and clung to their own conviction that they were uniquely qualified by vocation to supervise things related to writing. Yet Ebbitt was determined to unify the curriculum, to set up a strong central governing Freshman English Committee, and to establish ongoing staff meetings to invigorate pedagogy and to train a staff (many of whom were teaching assistants). Relentless, single-minded, serious, dedicated, and somewhat stern (though by no means humorless), she convinced Frank to support her initiatives and moved forthrightly to implement them. "Wilma is physically the smallest person, [. . .] but there is nobody in the world with a stronger will," said John Moore (personal interview). To assist her, Ebbitt recruited Douglas Park, an assistant professor who had joined the faculty in 1969 with a PhD from Cornell and a specialization in Restoration and eighteenth-century prose that gave him a natural interest in rhetoric and composition. With the department's support and encouragement Park spent a month in the summer of 1975 at Janice Lauer's summer seminar in composition at the University of Detroit.

Ebbitt and Park assembled on the Freshman English Committee a small group of faculty, nearly all of whom held PhDs (the Writing Option faculty were fairly completely excluded) and who had interest in and/or experience with composition issues. By the end of the summer of 1975, this committee had produced a set of principles and a draft curriculum that modified English 1 and drastically altered English 3. The reforms were signaled by a change in numbering as English 1 became English 10 and English 3 became English 20—two courses in a required and coordinated sequence, one course in exposition and one in argument.

The committee's work in reforming English 1 into English 10 was primarily a matter of consolidating instructors' approaches to a relatively uncontroversial curriculum based on the modes of expository prose. The course remained a series of traditional and conventional exercises in description, narration, process, analysis, comparison/contrast, and classification, all of it altered slightly in terms of the topics assigned and in order to incorporate a process approach to teaching writing.

More pressing was the need to reform English 3. English 3 (English 20)[45] was completely redesigned in stages after May of 1975, becoming both the counterpart to English 10, as part of a twenty-week sequence on exposition and argument, and a distinct course in argument in its own right.[46] While this initial change in 1975 was dramatic, it marked only the beginning of a two-year transformation culminating in a course in "argument and analysis" that in many respects still prevails today at Penn State. Between the summer of 1975 and the end of 1977, the new English 20 underwent extensive revision based on input from course instructors, the Freshman English Committee, and the new administrators of the program, who were in charge of renovating the curriculum and who were quite aware of national developments in composition studies. Responding to criticism that the previous literature-oriented English 3 was relevant to English majors alone, the new course explicitly set out to create a common curriculum to serve "every student enrolled in every college of the University," teaching skills that were necessary for "all modes of investigation and discussion" (Freshman English Committee "Proposal"). To the dismay of many instructors, even some who approved of the overall course renovations, the literature component of the course was eliminated completely—no more would the courses focus on the "great ideas" or "eternal values and themes" dramatized in literary masterpieces. Indeed, disturbed by evidence that English 3 had become a literature course and convinced by assumptions associated with literary modernism and New Criticism that the literary and the rhetorical were separate species of discourse, Ebbitt and her committee completely eliminated literary texts from English 1 and 3. They also discontinued the Minimum Essentials Test "since that practice seems to have been abused" (Ebbitt, "Memo to Arthur O. Lewis").

Designed around "modes of argument" (on the analogy with the "modes of exposition" emphasized in English 1/10), English 3/20 assumed that the subject matter of students' writing would come from their lives or their readings on mostly contemporary issues:

> What Doug [Park] and I [John Moore] were really pushing for was that what people were writing about was going to be stuff [problems and predicaments] in literature, the way I had been trained [at Stanford] and the way he [Park] had been trained at Cornell. [. . .] We ended up [in the final version of the new English 3] really assigning the method but not the problem, so I'd end up having to talk to people about [. . .]

> how many different types of shoes [they] have. [. . .] It seemed so basic. (Moore, personal interview)

Whether it was quite as basic as Moore recalls or not (Moore's description seems more an account of the fairly current-traditional English 1 than English 3, and betrays his political commitment to literature as the central content of English studies), the Freshman English Committee of 1975 did organize a seven-unit course to guide students through increasingly complex argumentative tasks. Students began by writing definitions and causal analyses, moved on to study interpretation and premises, and spent the final three units writing three types of rhetorically situated argument: an evaluation, a refutation, and a policy paper (Freshman English Committee, *English 1* 32–33). Rather than simply testing students' comprehension of dogmatic rules of good writing, the course presented students with "occasions" for employing rhetorical principles, giving students ample opportunity for "practice in finding evidence, sifting it, and marshaling it in support of a thesis; and [asking] them to construct arguments with a view to influencing the beliefs or actions of others" (35). Typical assignments crossed a broad spectrum of generic types, audiences, and objectives, including a personal essay on definition and causal analysis (e.g., "Why I Am What I Am"); a newspaper article interpreting an event (e.g., "the big game" or a campus social, political, or intellectual event); a response to an unenlightened friend, explaining and supporting or refuting some proposition (e.g., the inscription above the library doors, which reads, "The true university is a collection of books"); an evaluation of something (e.g., one's high school career, written at the request of the high school administration); and a policy argument proposing a specific course of action related to some issue under students' control. Although these assignments were rather artificial and though the course retained some vestiges of current traditionalism, the Freshman English Committee felt that creating a concrete rhetorical situation for student writing was more effective than simply offering literary texts and ideas for response. The course aimed at analysis and argumentation for civic and practical purposes: to teach students to engage in public debates, to change policies or shape courses of action, to discover the causes of everyday opinions and phenomena. And at least in principle, the assignments were sequenced so that each assignment would prepare the student for the next assignment. In the absence of an awareness of especially progressive scholarship on argument, the course stressed formal logic, the so-called logical fallacies, and rules of interpretation and evidence.

While the change from the old English 3 to the new English 3/20 curriculum was an important step, instructors and administrators alike nevertheless saw the 1975 syllabus as a rough draft, produced hastily in response to the several crises converging on the department and imposed on instructors prematurely. (That is why the Lindemann and Tate report referred to the syllabus as "transitional.") Ebbitt and the Freshman English Committee had to gather information on current practices, assess the situation, propose a response, and carry their ideas through department channels, all in a matter of months, so the results necessarily required revision. During the next few years, therefore, instructors and administrators, encouraged by Ebbitt and Park, contributed formally and informally to revisions which turned a rough collection of seven vaguely analytical and argumentative assignments into a sequence of argumentative elements with an arrangement both theoretically sound and responsive to the particular needs of students. Though these evolving revisions can be seen as responses to the local situations of students, instructors, and administrators, they also significantly paralleled disciplinary trends in composition studies—most important, attention to the composing process of writers, new regard for argument, and the increasing professionalization of composition theory, research, and pedagogy.

In 1975, the significance of recent research on the composing process had not really begun to register at Penn State. Ebbitt herself favored a large number of finished assignments over multiple revisions of fewer ones. That had substantially changed by 1977, in large part because of Park's experience at Janice Lauer's summer seminar, which certainly was attentive to new research on process. Although in 1975 some instructors did ask students to plan drafts, to practice peer review, and to revise their work, the departmental syllabus said very little about how these activities were to be taught or even about their importance for student writers. Most of the course attended to the components of solid finished arguments (evidence, premises, the process of formal reasoning, and so on), and to the technical correctness of students' prose, which was tested regularly through the institution of graded grammar quizzes. By 1977, the attention that the writing process was attracting in the profession was manifesting itself in several ways, both explicitly (through actual discussion of "process" in official documents) and implicitly (through changes in pedagogy and curriculum).

Indeed, the 1977 official departmental syllabuses featured a four-page section dealing with how to teach "the process of composing" in English 10 and 20, beginning with the premise that since writing was "a craft requiring a number of different skills, a process that takes place in stages, we ought to be able to show students how to get from one end of the process to the other" (*English 10* 9). Describing the writing process as a complex mix of physical, cognitive, and imaginative activities, the syllabus writers acknowledged that it is "so complexly various that we can never hope to teach it or coach students in it in any fully systematic way," and then charged instructors with developing strategies for guiding students through these processes, teaching them to discover and hone their processes for application in actual writing situations (*English 10* 9). This discussion of the pedagogy of process evidenced the composition program's new attention to composition as a research area. It explicitly cited Emig's 1971 study and two more recent studies of process pedagogy.[47] Attention to process appeared elsewhere in the syllabus as well, as instructors were encouraged to model writing in class and to design assignments with students' writing processes in mind.

Even more concretely, the influence of process pedagogy, through its cognitive and expressivist elements, affected both the way students at Penn State were asked to compose papers in their composition courses and the topics they were asked to address in assignments. By the fall of 1977, the structure of the assignments in English 10 reflected the department's growing interest in the cognitive processes involved in writing. The departmental handbook for English 10 that fall explained that "in English 10 the assignments largely grow from the basic ways the mind perceives and orders experience. The emphasis allows particular concentration on generating and ordering material" (*English 10* 1). While the principle underlying the order or the assignments reflected the cognitive emphasis of process pedagogy, the topics students were asked to write about reflected the expressivist belief that students should learn to write by writing about what they know. English 10 was designed to teach modes of exposition while also helping students develop authority and confidence in the writing process by using their experience as evidence in their papers. As the department handbook elaborated, "Having students write from their own experience guarantees that they have a large degree of control over and competence in the subject matter" (*English 10* 2).

Student papers composed for English 10 during this period reflect the priority given students' first-hand experience and expertise. For the description assignment, for example, students frequently focused on their hometowns or the interior of their Penn State dorm rooms. By asking students "to observe consciously and summon mental images of experience usually unnoticed, and [. . .] to convert those images into mental pictures" (*English 10* 23), instructors of English 10 collected papers that detailed scenes like the following:

> We have matching lemon yellow bedspreads which help pull together the lighter yellow of the walls and the yellow, brown, pink, and orange plaid curtains. Having yellow as the dominant color gives our room a bright, cheerful atmosphere.

or

> The two large windows on the southern and eastern parts of the room are of great benefit to the peeping tom across the street. They are covered with tedious, brown, flowered drapes, which irregularly match the ugly, plaid, plastic-covered cushions on the two sitting chairs.[48]

Similarly, the second assignment in the course, the narration paper, led several students in one section of English 10 to provide detailed accounts of fraternity parties they had attended. These papers took the audience, usually identified as "a friend from home," through a guided tour of the frat house on a weekend night, including details about the "wooden log split lengthwise, sanded, and heavily shellacked" that served as the bar; the "$300 worth of wine, vodka, beer, scotch, [and] bourbon" behind the bar; and the "life-sized posters of some of T.V.'s most popular female stars, such as Farrah Fawcett Majors, Suzanne Summers, Kate Jackson, and the Dallas Cowboy Cheerleaders." Penn State football games also served as the inevitable subject matter for narration papers, as students tried to convey, as one student put it, "the positive attitudes and the intense involvement that the students put forth toward football games."

Later, more complex assignments in the course also called for students to use their experiences as subject matter. The fifth paper in the fall 1977 course, for instance, asked students to produce an analysis of some phenomenon of which they had direct knowledge. The department handbook prompted instructors to have students analyze their responses to a recent television show or movie they had seen, to analyze the qualities of a person they consider a hero, or to analyze a custom or tradition they have practiced for several years (*English 10* 42). Sample student papers from this unit in one section—analyses of "my junior English class" and "the reasons why I went away to Penn State for school"—reflect the emphasis on valuing student experience. Other students relied on their experience of popular culture in their analysis papers. One student, for example, identified as his purpose "to analyze Crosby, Stills, and Nash's *CSN* album and persuade the audience that the album is in keeping with their high standards of music and social comment."

Even the last, and ostensibly the most complex, assignment in English 10 allowed students to work with their experience as subject matter. For their definition papers, students identified purposes such as "to define tailgating to my grandparents"; or to "define 4H" (a topic of significance to the many students in Penn State's College of Agriculture). Another student used popular media images to define the term "jet-set." Her definition relied on examples of famous people (Vitas Gerulaitis, Hugh Hefner, Liza Minelli, and Jackie Onassis), places (Studio 54), and fashion designs (Halston) that, she argued, exemplified the jet-set lifestyle.

The influence of process pedagogy also manifested itself in the increased amount of prewriting and drafting students were asked to do in English 10. In the spring of 1977, the Freshman English Committee established as the first two goals of English 10 "to develop awareness of the nature of the composing process and help students improve their own procedures for composing, [. . . and] to introduce the art of invention—techniques for helping students discover what they know and have to say, want to say, need to say" (*English 10* 4). To these ends, instructors were encouraged to have students work actively on invention techniques and multiple revision sessions in class. Influenced strongly by Emig's conclusion in *The Composing Processes of Twelfth Graders* that freshman English courses focused too often on editing and thus inhibited students' prewriting processes, the handbook for English 10 in 1977 urged instructors to remember that

> revising student writing in class [. . .] must show students that revising involves more than editing—which occupies a disproportionate and censorious place in most students' minds as the only thing English teachers really care about. We should show them by engaging them in it that we care equally about prewriting. (*English 10* 11)

Students were not the only ones required to engage in an extended writing process. By 1977, instructors were expected to participate in students' writing processes by providing considerable feedback on student work-in-progress. Student portfolios from one section of English 10 in the late 1970s contain multiple prewriting exercises, proposals, and multiple partial drafts on which the instructor provided feedback.

In terms of curriculum, the growing attention to the writing process also implicitly contributed to a very important change in the second required writing course, English 20: a move from seven writing assignments to five. Because instructors before 1975 focused mostly on characteristics of good written texts (and not on the processes involved in producing them), little time was needed, Ebbitt felt, between one finished text and the next. But as "pre-writing" (i.e., planning, invention, and arrangement) and revision practices demanded increased attention in class, instructors found that they needed more time for instruction before and after "final" drafts. By eliminating two of the seven formal assignments, instructors could spend an average of two weeks on each unit[49]; according to the syllabus, students spent much of that time writing preliminary texts "quickly and frequently," using exercises to learn particular techniques and working with rough drafts (their own and peers'). As attention to process was increasing, current-traditional attention to correctness and the mastery of Standard English faded somewhat. In the wake of "Students' Right to Their Own Language" and somewhat in the face of those who were inveighing for a return to basic skills, the number of grammar quizzes decreased, the Minimum Essentials Test was buried, and instructors were given more discretion about the content of grammar lessons and quizzes. Significantly, although the linguistic approaches to composition of the early 1970s apparently never took hold at Penn State in any direct or substantial way (though sentence combining made something of an appearance in the 1980s), attention to "syntactic fluency," so characteristic of transformational grammar, was a central stylistic concern in the 1977 syllabus.

Research in composition influenced English 20 in other ways, as well. The course was greatly influenced by the neo-Aristotelianism of the Chicago School that nurtured Wilma Ebbitt (as well as other faculty, such as Gus Kolich, who came to Penn State in 1977, and novelist Thomas Rogers) and by the work on the sources of argument of Richard Weaver, whom Ebbitt so greatly admired. The assignments for the course ultimately were arranged according to genres, since genre considerations were central to the Chicago School.[50] As attention to rhetorical situations and occasions for argumentation rose, the last vestiges of expressivism were abandoned in the official version of English 20, though those vestiges retained a toehold in some sections of the essentially unchanged English 10 and in some sections of the honors version of the freshman sequence, English 30.[51] Corbett's *Classical Rhetoric* was the most consistently referenced source in curricular support documents, though, except for style lessons, explicit borrowings from classical rhetoric were not really evident in course materials.

The interest in argument in the program also informed the work of then-lecturers Marie Secor and Jeanne Fahnestock, whose versions of the 1975–77 syllabi would firmly establish English 3/20 (after the example of English 10, which was organized around "the modes of exposition") as a course in the "modes of argument." Encouraged by the increased discussion among instructors and administrators in the composition program (Secor recalls of Park, "Bless his heart, he didn't say 'no' to the lecturers" [interview]), Fahnestock and Secor emerged from a staff meeting about English 3/20 with the kernels of the course that, although modified since, survives as the basis of the first-year course at Penn State today. As Secor explains,

> We were both teaching English 3/20. [. . .] We'd gone to a meeting where Doug was talking about an argument paper. [. . .] Jeanne and I came out of the meeting and said "No, no he's got it all wrong, Doug does. There are different kinds of arguments, they're not all the same." [At the meeting] everyone had submitted a topic assignment and we [Secor and Fahnestock]

> had those. We took them back [to our office] after the meeting and sorted them out. We said "Well, look, there are different kinds of arguments" [. . .]and we sorted them into different little piles [. . .] causal arguments, definition arguments [. . .] [and] proposals. It was like a moment that we figured that out. [. . .] Somehow we had come to this moment of clarity that there were different kinds of arguments and you can teach them differently.
>
> So we sat down and started doing the handout for the course. This was the handout that was going to lay out the different kinds of arguments and there would be different assignments corresponding to the different kinds of arguments. We gave that to Doug. [. . .] Doug looked at it and said "Yeah, that's it. That's good." [. . .] So he put us in charge of revising English 20 [. . .] even though we were still lecturers, in our attic office. (personal interview)

Thus, the 1975 hodge-podge of loosely argumentative and analytical assignments in English 3 became, by 1977, a carefully-ordered two-phase structured English 20, designed to introduce students first to the "logical underpinnings" of argument and then to the actual uses of argument in rhetorical situations. Together, units one and two dealt with "Evidence" and "Premises of Positive Argument," collectively described in the syllabus as "the logical underpinnings of argument" (*English 20* 5). Then students were to experiment "with the common sources of argument—definition, cause and effect, comparison, testimony and authority"—sources which were drawn more or less directly from Richard Weaver and his colleagues' "Looking for an Argument" (Bilsky et al. 210). Following this training, students would write another "Positive Argument." The goal of the first three assignments was to give students multiple opportunities to apply what they were learning about argument, and these assignments were expected to become more complex as students learned more about the sources and bases of argument. So, for instance, in Assignment 3, students might tackle a proposal or evaluation argument, drawing upon what they had learned about value, authority, evidence, deduction, and so on. Whereas this initial three-unit section of the course dealt with argument in the abstract, divorced from specific rhetorical situations, the fourth and fifth assignments made the leap into more distinctly rhetorical situations, explicitly placing students "in a rhetorical situation where attention to audience is a major and unavoidable issue" (*English 20* 5). The fifth assignment in particular brought together all the lessons of the semester and asked students to deploy them in a specfic rhetorical situation by refuting a fully-developed argument.

With the 1977 syllabus, then, English 20 had fully become the course in argument that Ebbitt and her associates had only begun to envision in 1975. The sequence of assignments reflected the composition program's argument-centered, rhetorically based, process-oriented philosophy of composition, responding directly to several currents of theoretical inquiry that had begun making their way into the program in the mid-1970s. In the words of Doug Park, "Research in the teaching of writing is blooming all over the country; our syllabi should reflect our share of the activity" (Park, "Memo to Instructors"). On the basis of their work with the 1977 syllabus, Marie Secor and Jeanne Fahnestock began to hatch plans for an argument textbook that would serve the course and that would appeal as well to teachers across the country who were turning toward argument, *A Rhetoric of Argument* (first published in 1982). And a committee developed a reader that was specifically tied to the course goals, with sections of essays that illustrated "Supporting Generalizations," "Interpreting Evidence," "Arguing from Premises to Conclusions," "Analyzing Issues and Arguing," and "Refuting and Arguing" (*The Penn State Reader: 20,* ed. Douglas Park and Edward Uehling, first published in 1977).

In sum, therefore, while English 10 had asked students to examine and explain their experiences of college life and popular culture, English 20 asked them to research carefully, to think critically, and to argue meaningfully about the world around them. The first English 20 department handbook clarified the differences between the two courses thus: While in English 10 "the subjects for writing should come largely from the student's own experience and knowledge," in English 20 "the subjects for writing may depend more upon the reading that students do. [. . . T]he greater complexity of the assignments will demand information that usually only reading can provide. Some of the assignments [. . .] should require students to analyze and respond to the writing of others" (*English 20* 1–2). To help students write their way into contemporary conversations through analysis and argument, the department suggested that English 20 should ask students to

1. develop various kinds of evidence in support of propositions: fully developed illustrations, statistics, quotations, sensory detail [. . .];
2. interpret and analyze a body of evidence, drawing from it well-supported and developed inferences and conclusions;
3. develop, define, and establish premises in support of a judgment or proposal;
4. summarize a fully developed argument, maintaining the structure, emphasis, and proportion of the original;
5. analyze and discuss the issues present in a given problem, situation, or body of argument;
6. analyze and refute another fully stated argument
7. wherever possible, specify and write to a well-defined audience and occasion. (*English 20* 1–2)

As part of this plan to make English 20 a course in research and argument, assignments no longer focused on literary readings. Rather, students were asked to investigate and compose arguments about pressing, current, controversial issues. Student papers collected at the time frequently address relevant campus controversies, such as inequalities in tuition assessment for in-state residents; the relative merits of a ten-week and fifteen-week academic semester (Penn State was in the middle of a switch from the former to the latter); the need for greater privacy in dorm living arrangements; and "conflicts [. . .] between the Greek and Independent students at colleges and universities." Many students also addressed national and international political controversies of the day. One student wrote a paper refuting an editorial in the *Harrisburg Patriot* which had criticized President Carter's proposed tax on oil company profits. Other students, reflecting a different political persuasion, argued for a decrease in federal income tax for wealthy Americans and against proposed federal minimum wage legislation. Still others addressed issues of public health or safety in which they were particularly interested, such as the benefits of organized sports for children or the environmental dangers of strip mining.

Student essays submitted in these early sections of English 20 often reflected the results of extensive research; their bibliographies included multiple news sources. While many students consulted the mainstream media (e.g. *Esquire, Reader's Digest, Fortune, Time,* and

Newsweek), several others engaged more specialized publications. One student—who chose to write one of his arguments to the editors of *Easy Rider* advocating stiffer motorcycle helmet laws—included extensive statistical evidence from a Department of Transportation study of crash-related fatalities and from a study conducted by the Acoustical Society of America on the impact of helmets on riders' hearing. While the student consulted several mainstream publications, such as *Newsweek* and *U.S. News & World Report,* he also consulted more specialized sources, including *Cycle* and *Technology Review,* in order to obtain a breadth of perspective in gathering evidence and refuting claims. The student who argued for changes in minimum wage legislation sought non-mainstream perspectives through readings in the *Navajo Times.*

Inventing Basic Writing, Reorganizing the Writing Center

Curricular change was not limited to English 10 and 20, however. In addition to revising English 1 and 3 (into English 10 and 20) to address local concerns and accommodate national developments in scholarship, Penn State's University Park campus also responded to the public's demands that students be more thoroughly educated in basic skills. And they did so in keeping with national developments in basic writing.

In 1974, a year before the publication of "Why Johnny Can't Write" in *Newsweek,* Martha Kolln, a Penn State linguist, had been called upon to devise and teach a new course called "English 4—Basic Writing," a preliminary course to English 1. (The number was logical in that English 1, 2, and 3 were then the established courses in the composition sequence.) Kolln, who had taught part-time for some years and was just going onto the tenure line, was chosen because of her linguistic training: "Because I was teaching the grammar course [English 100, required for education majors], it was assumed that I would [. . .] know how to teach remedial English because most people think of the grammar course as a remedial course [though] it isn't" (personal interview). True to her linguistic training and current-traditional custom, Kolln prepared a syllabus for English 4 during 1974–75 (it was offered first in 1975–76) that concentrated mostly on grammar—on sentence-level correctness and sentence structure. Her students focused on the grammatical elements of sentences: achieving subject-verb agreement and tense consistency, avoiding fragments, combining sentences effectively, and so on.

Her syllabus was used for just one year before Harvey Wiener arrived at University Park in the fall of 1976, newly hired and charged with revamping the English 4 course in response to the basic skills initiatives that were animating the campus. Wiener remembered the "crisis" atmosphere under which he worked: "I figured out why they needed me—there was a serious basic writing issue on the branch campuses, not so serious an issue on the main campus, and they wanted me to do a [. . .] basic writing curriculum" (personal interview). Wiener had been working with Mina Shaughnessy in New York City, as we have indicated, and so he brought with him Shaughnessy's most current philosophies about basic writers, notably an emphasis on daily writing and an enlightened attitude about error. Kolln remembers now with a smile that Wiener "took a look at my syllabus and just *blanched*" because he "couldn't believe that anyone would be trying to teach basic writers by using only grammar" (personal interview). Wiener reflected on this stance in the introduction to his later publication *The Writing Room* (1981), a product of his work at Penn State: "I have found that 'remedial' students suffer daily doses of run-ons and apostrophes as the program of cure for sick writers. [. . .] In only some cases was frequent writing demanded of the student" (7). His course would instead emphasize, in Shaughnessy's manner, weekly writing of 1000–1500 words.

Wiener stayed at the University Park campus for just one year, during which time he worked to design an English 4 curriculum that would be useful to the entire PSU system, the Commonwealth Campuses as well as University Park. Recalling that time, Wiener compared University Park to CUNY: at PSU "the seriousness of the issue of basic writing hadn't quite caught up with them and as a result it was easy to ignore the problems" (personal interview). According to Wiener, Wilma Ebbitt and Doug Park were instrumental in bringing him to Penn State to design the new syllabus: their main concern, according to Wiener, was to stabilize the situation at the Commonwealth Campuses.[52] According to official university figures, 256 of the 1697 students who were required to take basic writing at Penn State in the first semester of the 1977–78 academic year were enrolled at University Park (Senate Special Committee, "Basic Skills," Appendix F). The others were on the two-year campuses.

Wiener's syllabus, which he ultimately turned into his book *The Writing Room,* centered around the paragraph rather than the sentence:

> The formal writing I suggest focuses on the paragraph and upon experiments with three basic types—description, narration, and illustration—only because they are easily accessible to inexperienced writers and because they are vehicles of practice for basic language skills and for skills in organization, in form, in the use of detail, and in correctness. (*Writing Room* 8)

Rather than starting with a current-traditional emphasis on correctness, a move that he believed often paralyzed inexperienced writers, Wiener suggested that as students became comfortable with their writing in a certain generic form, they would be better able to focus on correctness:

> I was trying to move people away from the grammar, fill-in-the-blank idea. [. . .] I have a philosophy of teaching [. . .] which is rooted in experiential exploration that ultimately moves students into other kinds of writing. [. . .] What I felt I was able to do with my program was to teach students about supporting detail. To expect them to be able to make an assertion with data-driven information or the abstractions that come from reading and putting ideas together I felt was premature. [Instead I] ask a student to develop an assertion on some element of his life and [. . .] teach a student how to use concrete sensory details, then later make the transition from sensory language to other kinds of language—statistics, cases, quotations, expert testimony. So the course was pretty much grounded in that philosophy evolving from the use of sensory language and descriptive and narrative moves to a kind of transition point in teaching examples and then showing students the use of data and then moving on to other forms of writing, having expanded the storehouse of options. (personal interview)

The resulting course focused almost solely on student writing—outside texts were approved but specified as "supplemental": "The book is an adjunct to the course. It is not the course itself" ("Basic Writing" VII: 100). Students generated a good deal of writing, and sometimes they would read their pieces in class in order to receive feedback from their classmates, as in the workshop model used in creative writing courses.

According to Kolln (who may well be understating her own contributions), the small group of instructors who taught basic writing at University Park (Ebbitt was one of them) welcomed Wiener's syllabus: none of them claimed to be expert teachers, and so Wiener's guidance was much appreciated. The resource book for basic writing instructors provided a proposed daily schedule, a breakdown and explanation of each assignment, and suggestions for error-elimination activities (for even Shaughnessy's approach was to a large degree concerned with error). In addition to this thorough course outline, the basic writing instructors at University Park met weekly with Wiener to discuss the week's lesson plans as well as to consider methods of assessing student writers: "We went through the papers together, and tried to come up with a grade we would agree on. [We discussed] what you would mark and what you would suggest for how to improve," Kolln explained (personal interview). Wiener was very available to help basic writing instructors better understand the writers with whom they would be working; Diane Greenfield, a tutor in the writing center from 1976 to 1983, years later still remembered his energy and enthusiasm—and his "optimism about his students" (personal interview).

However, relatively few instructors at University Park—about a half dozen—were actually involved in basic writing, mostly because at the University Park campus basic writing was less of an issue than at others. And at University Park there was also some antipathy to the very notion of "basic writing." Some faculty in English and other fields believed, predictably, that remediation was not the responsibility of the university and resisted the faculty senate initiatives on remediation. Others resisted the involvement of the English department and its resources in such an effort. Wiener still recalls one particular event that demonstrated the hostility he experienced for some of his efforts with basic writers: "I wrote an article for the newspaper [. . .] about the concept of remediation. I'd always opposed that as a construct and that was unfortunately the way it was defined at Penn State, as a remedial effort. [. . .] [The article] was about why we shouldn't be thinking about this as a remedial effort. It [was] printed and two or three months later [. . .] Bob [Frank] call[ed] me to the office. One of the senior lit faculty had sent him a blue-penciled copy [. . .] circling the errors and bad locutions. To Bob, this was a very serious issue. [. . .] That's when I decided I'd better get out of there. The support was not [forthcoming . . .] so I left" (personal interview).[53]

As for the actual basic writing course, it required completion of a minimum of eight long paragraphs, beginning with description, moving to narration, and ending with illustration. These paragraphs were to be 10–15 sentences or 200–250 words long, admittedly not the length of "normal" paragraphs encountered in the daily newspaper or other works students might read. Wiener defended his choices: "At this stage of development the paragraph of substance is the best way to teach required skills of invention, detail, and correctness within some structure that serves the writer's purpose" ("Basic Writing" I: 5). The first paragraphs assigned encouraged focused description, usually of a particular person or place, at a specific moment. When students moved on to narration, their topics were strictly focused here as well, often to a particular moment in time rather than spanning a day or even an hour. Class activities both utilized peer feedback, in-class discussion, or peer review, and stressed process pedagogy through the working of several drafts, beginning with brainstorming and ending with proofreading. By the end of the semester, students were supposed to understand the usefulness of invention and the importance of sustained and interconnected detail in their writing. Their chance to prove their knowledge arrived with their final paragraph-length assignment, an in-class assignment on a "new" topic.

This "final exam" for English 4 was for many reasons problematic in terms of the pedagogy of English 4: it allowed only compressed time for composition; it rejected a sense of progress for each student (in that a student's progress over a semester was not even considered when the student was being passed on—or not—to English 1/10); and "finally, and perhaps most important, the in-class theme on an unannounced topic fl[ew] in the face of everything we [were] teach[ing] about the writing process: that writing is a slow activity and must take time; that writers think and jot down notes and alter these notes until they produce a piece of writing that is logical, clear, and correct" ("Basic Writing" III: 58). Despite these failings, the final exit theme was defended in the instructors' resource book: "One reason [for keeping the exam] is that the Administration insists, as part of the new legislation on the basic skills effort, that each course build in an evaluation technique. Unless we require a writing sample, we shall no doubt have to settle for a multiple choice horror which insists upon valid correlations but which asks for no writing at all" (III: 59). Clearly, encouraging students to "speed up" their writing process was preferable to returning to a grammar-based exam. Thus, students on each campus were brought together at the end of English 4 to write on one of three topics, representing each of the paragraph types the students had been taught over the course of the semester.

The issues raised by an exit exam for English 4 troubled the Commonwealth Campuses and Kolln as well. The grading was intended to be "scientific" because this exam was part of the push for quantifiable data, which was encouraged by the University's Basic Skills Committee, especially its coordinator, educational psychologist Helen Snyder. These exams were rated according to four categories: meaning and idea, structure, mechanics, and language. Greenfield recalls that short student essays were graded holistically by groups of instructors who were conscious of maintaining standards; at least two teachers scored each essay, and a third was used to resolve differences (personal interview). Kolln recalled that, usually, the number of grammatical "errors" made the largest difference in the rating of the student's essay. Kolln stated that some errors were more serious than others, but seven or more errors meant that students flunked the entire course. Kolln also remembers some students having to take the course two or three times (personal interview).[54]

Kolln and Wiener were also involved in a "revision" of the Writing Center at University Park. Wiener remembers his first impression of the Writing Center, which he called more of a "grammar center" (the legacy of its function in helping students through the Minimum Essentials Test): "I'll never forget. [. . . T]here was a cartoon [hanging up] with someone lying in a hospital bed and a nurse and the sign said 'We fix sick sentences'" (personal interview). The "Writing Clinic" that Wiener encountered had been around for years, but Wiener made immediate changes that reflected developments at other universities. The name "Writing Clinic" was immediately discarded in favor of "Writing Center" (Greenfield, interview; she was the founding director of the facility). Furthermore, recalls Wiener, "We established the idea of process, invited faculty from all the departments, and we reported back to them" (personal interview). Surely this focus on accountability stemmed from concerns expressed by other departments that English was not being taught effectively in the first-year courses. Kolln also remembers the Writing Center, such as it was: "We did have drop-in hours and we also had scheduled hours. [. . . I]t wasn't a very elaborate setup. It was a room downstairs and it had cubbies [i.e., cubbyholes, or small carrels where tutors worked with students]. [. . .] Students just came in and signed up" for tutorials (personal interview). Many of these students would have been basic writers seeking additional help with their paragraphs, and instructors in the center worked closely with them, brainstorming, outlining, and teaching grammatical concepts when necessary. A December 15, 1978 memo from Kolln to composition teachers indicates that tutors were now thinking of themselves not as language police but as "trained and sympathetic reader[s]"; tutors communicated regularly with teachers, emphasized the strong points in student writing, and "deal[t] with student writing [. . .] as a whole." (Memo). By engaging students in dialogue about their writing, Writing Center tutors sought to make students more self-sufficient (Greenfield, personal interview).

By the end of 1977, developments in English 4 and in the Writing Center were fully sanctioned and officially supported by the university. The Basic Skills Committee recommended the continuation of English 4 and additional funding for the Writing Center, which would serve students from all departments. In addition, the Basic Skills Committee insisted that students demonstrate mastery of pre-college writing skills by earning a score high enough on the university placement exam. (The exam consisted of 120 multiple-choice questions: 31 or fewer correct answers defined a student as "deficient"; although some students managed to pass the placement exam on a second try, the majority of "deficient" students "removed their deficiency" by taking English 4 and passing the exit exam.[55]) Harvey Wiener left Penn State after just one year, and left with a sense of frustration at how he had been welcomed by some colleagues in English; but he and Martha Kolln had effected improvements in basic writing and the University Writing Center that were indelible.

Administrative Improvements

The faculty senate's interest in the Writing Center and in basic skills curricula was only one part of an institutional effort at Penn State to answer questions related to composition in the English department in the mid-1970s. Other administrative changes within English were designed to alleviate various problems associated with instruction in first-year composition courses.

The most pressing need seemed to be for better teacher training—something of a challenge given the shortage of faculty with formal training and interest in composition pedagogy. As we mentioned previously, before the mid-1970s at Penn State, graduate students teaching freshman composition received little or no formal training, in keeping with professional opinion that "anyone could teach composition" (Frank, personal interview). Teaching in particular courses tended to proceed according to the style of whomever happened to be the reigning course directors, according to one former director, S. Leonard Rubinstein (personal interview). That is, teachers were offered booklists and course overviews prepared by previous instructors, and an informal network of collaborative discussion about the courses stood for supervision. Novice teaching assistants were assigned to faculty mentors, who offered what assistance they could and cared to give (Frank, personal interview). Because the system originally developed when staff members were mainly tenure-line faculty, the habit developed of letting instructors find their own means of achieving course goals. But after speaking with other professors present during this period, we discovered that graduate-student teachers were sometimes left bewildered at the task before them; some graduate students even skipped or canceled classes out of frustration over what to teach and the lack of active supervision.

In response to the apparent need for guidance for beginning composition teachers, several procedures were implemented to conventionalize the teaching process and bring a measurable standard of instruction to the composition program. A full two-day orientation, reminiscent of programs at Ohio State and elsewhere, began in 1977 for new teaching assistants to ground them in some of the fundamentals of composition, instill confidence, and prepare them for the unique challenges of college instruction.[56] In his comments in the university's faculty newsletter, then English department head Robert Frank likened teaching assistants to medical interns in that they were learning to teach through active practice ("Point of View" 1). The teaching assistants met frequently to discuss classroom approaches and teaching techniques (DuBois). Faculty observations of student-instructors, end-of-course instructor evaluations, and a more standardized curriculum (with an organized structure for proposing alternative teaching methods) were among the accountability techniques employed for the first time in 1977 and 1978. There were even occasional general gatherings to discuss pedagogical matters of one kind of another, and colloquia presentations on the subject of composition. Frank, for instance, invited Wallace Douglas to visit the department from Northwestern University for two days to discuss the importance of composition reforms, and we have already mentioned the visit of Erika Lindemann and Gary Tate. The English department occasionally invited non-English faculty to lead presentations (e.g., faculty in education spoke about classroom management) both as a means of providing diversified viewpoints on English instruction and as a good will gesture to showcase the changes in composition and to diffuse dissatisfaction with the composition program.

Additionally, for experienced teachers the English department organized course-specific staff meetings to debate teaching techniques and classroom strategies, after the example of the famous staff meetings that Wilma Ebbitt had participated in for years at the University of Chicago. Because nearly no one at this point had previously taught the newly organized courses, particularly the new English 20, and because many faculty were moving once again into composition classrooms, these groups were engaging and fruitful, according to Nancy Lowe (personal interview); Robert Frank too recalls that the meetings "created a lot of [intellectual] excitement" (personal interview). At each meeting, "somebody would be designated the leader" and the group would then grapple with details regarding each unit, the readings, and how to manage exercises, according to Lowe. Communication among instructors and members of the administration was improved, and the consequence was that the conduct of English 10 and 20 also improved and disparate teaching methods became more consistent from section to section. The separate courses were cohering into an actual "program."[57]

Penn State also began encouraging specific coursework in composition for graduate students to further ground them in the fundamentals of the subject. Under the guidance of Doug Park, the department in 1977 began to require teaching assistants to take specific graduate coursework in composition theory: English 502, The Theory and Teaching of Composition, a three-credit seminar (offered first under an "experimental" number, English 597) that some saw as a foundation course that would run parallel to the required introductory seminar in research methods, English 501. According to Park, "the purpose of the course was to provide some theory to back up the discussions of practice that were going on in the staff meetings. The staff meetings, of course, were limited to purely practical teaching issues, sharing assignments, etc." In 1977 Park attempted to use the course to familiarize teaching assistants with the scholarly work on basic writing and composition pedagogy just becoming available and popular. "We spent some time with *Errors and Expectations* and related material on understanding error in student writing," he recalls. He also recalls that the course focused on work that questioned previous models of correctness and Standard English: "We got into some sociolinguistics and the history of prescriptive grammar. I remember wanting to do what I could to unstick some of those rigid ideas about correctness that new teachers are likely to be attached to." Park also introduced the emergent theories of process to the course that he had learned about during Janice Lauer's summer institute—though he was "thoroughly skeptical about the way she approached invention" (Park, email to Wendy Sharer).

Countercurrents and Counterattacks

Park, Ebbitt, Frank, and other leaders wanted the three-credit English 502 to remain a required course for all graduate students in English, but that recommendation was voted down by the graduate faculty in the spring of 1978. English 502 remained an elective offering, and the department instead instituted a requirement for English 602, a two-credit, year-long weekly staff meeting for new teachers of composition that focused on pedagogy. Park still feels that a required English 502 made sense and that it was prevented from becoming a requirement because many faculty resented the increased administrative oversight that had emerged in the composition program and resisted the decision to remove English and American literature from the composition curriculum: "There was a lot of division in the department at that time about the amount of structure we had introduced into the program and about the exclusion of literature" (email to Wendy Sharer). The independent evaluation of the English program submitted in October of 1977 by Erika Lindemann and Gary Tate provided additional recommendations for improvements to the conditions under which composition teachers were working, and those recommendations were pursued despite opposition. Some of the suggestions—including reducing class size to no more than 25 students (the official size was then 28, but enrollment commonly ballooned to 30 or more [Ebbitt, "Memo to Arthur O. Lewis"]), safeguards to prevent grade inflation, expansion of the mandatory basic writing requirements, and less dependence on part-time instructors—were relatively uncontroversial. Though changes in class size were not forthcoming for several years, the English department did retain a significant number of faculty lines, accrued through retirements, to deal specifically with the issues of remediation and composition: besides the short-term addition of Harvey Wiener, the department acquired four faculty in composition who began tenure-line appointments in September, 1978. Those lines were relatively uncontroversial too because literature faculty did not especially want new hires to compete for diminishing literature offerings.

But other moves, like the proposal to require English 502, met with resistance. Composition did not operate autonomously, nor were the changes in the program received with a great deal of enthusiasm. To start, composition was still very much a "stepchild" of the department, according to Martha Kolln (personal interview). The sudden rise in the importance of composition instruction brought with it uneasiness over the accompanying program revisions. Because Wilma Ebbitt was at the center of these changes, she received considerable disapprobation. Other professors "hated" the new curriculum and Ebbitt herself, according to Marie Secor (personal interview). "We were all mocked in those days for [. . .] admiring Wilma. It was a mark of shame to be on her side on anything," Secor said. Maxwell adds,

> I think faculty belly-ached a lot more under [Ebbitt] than they did under the old system, because under the old system you could do pretty much what you wanted. But when Wilma came she was saying "This is a program, not just two or three course chairmen. [. . .] We've got a comp director and we have a theory of composition and we've got a curriculum." (personal interview)

Ebbitt brought a sense of structure that some faculty members deemed tyrannical, especially faculty members who weren't much interested in composition but who were now being encouraged or required to teach a section, and Ebbitt's approach to the curriculum was indeed uncompromising. Her gender no doubt worked against her as well, though she made alliances with a great many influential men. But many people, including some in powerful positions, regarded Ebbitt's rigidity as a necessary evil—a transition to a logical focus out of an undefined, loosely controlled approach to composition instruction. And many others found her to be an inspiring role model and unforgettable teacher (see, for example, Eberly), one who was chosen twice to be faculty marshall at graduation by the leading student in the College of Liberal Arts, who won the University's Amoco Outstanding Teaching Award in 1984, and who was named a Penn State teaching fellow—an honored teacher of teachers—in 1987, just before her retirement.

Many professors interested in literary studies resisted change because they wanted composition to serve as an introduction to and recruiting ground for literary studies in a time when literature enrollments were down, according to Secor (personal interview); and, as Sharon Crowley emphasizes in chapter five of *Composition in the University,* the issue of literature in the composition course has from the beginning been bound up in the more general question of the professional identity of English studies. The perception was that the new composition program had become a lowly, remedial-based service operation that was taught without content ("content" being nearly synonymous with "literature"), and that the literature faculty members were forced to teach it in spite of their histories and better judgments. Meanwhile, creative writing faculty were committed to less formalized, workshop-oriented approaches to the teaching of writing that were inattentive to rhetorical theory and composition pedagogy; their courses implicitly commented on the new composition initiatives. Creative writing faculty, raised like their rivals in literary studies on New Critical attitudes to rhetoric as ephemeral, degraded, and therefore unworthy of advanced study (while literature was regarded as the eloquent articulation of transcendent values), also were by nature suspicious of rhetoric as a foundation for composition. Convinced that rhetoric and composition were less relevant to the preparation of writers than were practical experience and the example of outstanding instances, the creative writers upheld the value of literary masterpieces to the teaching of writing. Many of them, including Peter Schneeman, supported the use of "casebooks" in the composition classroom (personal interview). These casebooks—collections of sequentially structured readings, nearly always literary in nature, on given themes (e.g., one was on Hiroshima)—if used strictly in the context of composition rather than solely as a study of literature, provided, they felt, the necessary content to open up student ideas and humanized the approach to writing. In Rubinstein's composition model, literary readings provided the framework for class discussion, and students would use the discussions to frame essays ("Composition: A Collision" 273). When these readings were eliminated, many faculty felt that substantial content was eliminated as well: students chose their own paper topics and were accused of writing about things like "why Izod shirts are better than the off-brand," according to Schneeman (and without doubt some instructors did invite such papers in English 10). Form was the emphasis in the new composition and content was removed, critics charged. "It was a dumbing-down. Writing what you know without thinking," contends Schneeman (personal interview). Rubinstein saw the new program as a means to the same end as the old—making better writers—but explained that the discourse of rhetoric introduced a professional, academic vocabulary that was incomprehensible to the average college student. It was the language of PhD candidates, he felt as a writer, a language that was "far in excess" of the one needed to teach students to write (personal interview).[58]

Additionally, Ebbitt's strict enforcement of the composition regimen developed tension among experienced faculty members still subscribing to the traditional method of teaching composition; it was sometimes difficult for instructors used to making their own decisions to become excited about teaching a standard composition syllabus. If there's one thing you can't do to faculty members, it's to tell them "this is how you are going to teach the course," explained Moore (personal interview). Many faculty members openly attacked the new program and curriculum while others simply refused to participate in the planning process as it violated their personal beliefs about composition instruction (Schneeman, personal interview). Faculty from the Commonwealth Campuses especially spoke out in opposition to what they perceived as impositions made by the University Park faculty, particularly because they had been involved in devising their own professionalized composition courses in response to the arrival of the "new students" of the 1970s. As John Moore recalls,

> In the fall of 1975, there was a meeting of the entire English department—[including] all of the people from the Commonwealth Campuses in 112 Kern [Building . . .] The members of the [Freshman English] Committee were sitting in the front. I remember [. . .] people from the Commonwealth Campuses yelling and screaming at us because we were basically imposing a fixed syllabus. I remember one woman from Ogontz [Campus] got up and said to [Ebbitt], "Thou shalt not impose this text on us" and Wilma responded with something like "Well, that's just what we're doing." (personal interview)

Some of the weekly staff meetings were equally "ferocious" because "Wilma was insisting on definition and, like any good rhetorician ,refusing to use persuasion, instead using force to get her way," said John Moore with a wry smile. Ultimately, as a result of all this pressure Wilma Ebbitt resigned her post as composition director in the summer of 1976 after just over one year—though she succeeded in having Park named director and thus remained very closely identified with the program. Newly hired compositionists soon took over other leadership positions, permitting Ebbitt to return to fulltime teaching (mainly in American literature and in editing, one of her special talents), but she remained interested and involved in composition until her retirement in 1989. (She passed away in September, 2000.)

As traditionalists resisted changes in the first-year writing program, sometimes vigorously, so too traditionalists remained in charge of the curricula in technical writing and business writing. In fact, technical and business writing were considered to be operations quite separate from composition in 1977 at Penn State, and operations that were in the hands of people who had taught the courses responsibly for years. Robert Weaver, a versatile writer and teacher whose *Persuasive Writing: A Manager's Guide to Effective Letters and Reports* appeared in 1977; James Holahan, who had worked as a technical writer in industry; and William Damerst, a full professor who had written a textbook on technical writing (*Clear Technical Reports*, 1972), were all tenured if nearing retirement. Recently retired was Kenneth Houp, who had originally coauthored Thomas Pearsall's *Reporting Technical Information,* but who had dropped out of the new third edition that was published in 1977 and that was sensitive to new directions in writing pedagogy.[59] And a recent arrival was James Hill, an assistant professor who joined the faculty in 1974 after many years as a technical writer. None of those held the PhD, but all except Hill had contributed to the department's Writing Option for many years. Perhaps because they had not pursued advanced graduate study, but also because they were regarded as successful at their trades as writers, they tended to offer time-honored curricula in technical and business writing—courses that took students through somewhat stereotypical assignments (often based on case studies); that were inattentive to new approaches to teaching the composing process; that regarded invention as the province not of writing teachers but of those in engineering, agriculture, science, and industry; that featured positivistic assumptions about language (for instance, by emphasizing usage, correctness, formulaic rules, and readability formulas); and that depended on current-traditional textbooks (the 1970 third edition of Gordon Mills and John Walter's *Technical Writing,* Damerst's *Clear Technical Reports,* Herta Murphy and Charles Peck's *Effective Business Communications,* or even the 1977 edition of Walter Wells's *Communications in Business,* which owed more than a little to the field of secretarial science).

Those courses served well enough when relatively few students enrolled in technical and business communication and when experienced faculty covered nearly every section of introductory and advanced technical and business writing. As the so-called literacy crisis deepened in the mid-1970s, however, more students were encouraged or even required to take business and technical writing. Holahan in 1977 began offering a training program for new teachers, therefore, that used not the model of English 602—a once-a-week hourly seminar for new teachers—and certainly not a system of staff meetings (which Writing Option faculty ridiculed), but rather an apprenticeship based on the example of multi-section literature classes: all students in the multi-section technical writing course came together for large lectures once a week by Holahan, and then met twice a week with individual (new) instructors, who guided assignments to completion with the help of models and who then graded the assignments. For several years technical and business writing remained separate from composition at

Penn State (as at many institutions). The business writing and technical writing staffs worked out of a different set of assumptions and were unengaged by the American Business Communication Association, the Association of Teachers of Technical Writing, and CPTSC—until in the early 1980s, when the director of composition also assumed responsibility for technical and business writing.

Postscript: Two Conclusions

Technical and business writing remained in the hands of the traditionalists at Penn State, and those traditionalists resisted the reforms of the mid-1970s, as best they could, for some years after. But in many ways, the opposition had lost. Though many faculty at University Park and the Commonwealth Campuses for the next decade resisted to varying degrees the reforms of the mid-1970s, over the long term what the winners called "reforms" carried the day. By the end of 1977, Penn Staters had devised, out of a rather grand debate about a local crisis, a rather different composition program, one that amounted to a sustained professional response to a challenging set of new circumstances—circumstances nonetheless comparable to those in many other places and influenced by developments, intellectual and otherwise, around the country. There was still plenty of work to be done, of course, especially on English 20, the new argument course that needed refinement, but also on English 10, which had been fairly well ignored in the controversy over basic skills and the switch to an argument-based English 20, but which was beginning to creak under its current-traditional assumptions. And there was a need for professional development at the graduate level.

By the fall of 1978, however, Frank, Ebbitt, and Park had arranged for four new tenure-line faculty to work on the problems. Marie Secor and Jeanne Fahnestock, having worked with Park and Ebbitt for several years, were promoted from the fixed-term faculty to the tenure track—Secor with a doctoral degree from Brown and Fahnestock with one from the University of London, and both of them with interests in Victorian fiction, language and style, and of course argument. Betsy Brown, Andrea Lunsford's close friend at Ohio State and another protégé of Edward Corbett, came to Penn State with special expertise in basic writing and in first-year composition—and a special understanding of how to make curricula workable throughout a large multi-section program. Jack Selzer was hired out of Miami University, where his studies of the English Renaissance had introduced him to the history of rhetoric, where he had observed Daiker, Kerek, and Morenberg's work on sentence combining, and where he had been introduced to process-based approaches to the teaching of technical writing by Paul Anderson. Doug Park would leave Penn State in 1979, in part because he had an opportunity to be a department chair at Western Washington University, but he was replaced as director temporarily by Fahnestock and then by another new faculty member, John Harwood, who had been a member of James Sledd's NEH seminar on language diversity while he worked on his doctorate in eighteenth-century English drama. And so the reforms remained in place—a foundation to maintain and build on. By the spring of 1978, matters had been resolved at Penn State, for better or for worse, in a way that would last for five years, until a change from the ten-week term calendar to a fifteen-week semester calendar in the early 1980s prompted additional revisions. Those revisions, governed by insights gained by the invention of the Penn State Conference on Rhetoric and Composition in 1981—as well as by professional concerns and developments elsewhere in the field, in higher education, and in the culture at large—created still further turns at Penn State and in the United States in the conflicted but invigorating cultural conversation that we know as composition.

Or so it is possible to say. The story of composition at Penn State in the 1970s can be read as a narrative of progress, a story of barriers overcome, improvements instituted, changes successfully negotiated. But there is another way of interpreting the events we have recounted, one that is not so happy. Tom Rogers, a senior fiction writer who was actively involved in English department deliberations during the 1970s, including curricular discussions about composition courses, regards the changes instituted in 1977 with ambivalence. "I wouldn't argue against [the] judgment that the reforms started by Wilma [Ebbitt] and carried forward by Doug Park [. . .] and others have greatly improved our composition program," Rogers now believes (personal correspondence). But those reforms also came, he feels (and with reason), at the expense and diminution and marginalization of the Writing Option in English and of the subsequent MFA program in writing that was associated with the Writing Option. "Rhetoric has triumphed," Rogers notes,

> But creative writing has faltered. [. . .] Their last shot came when Bob Frank created a committee [in 1976 or 1977] to assess and revise the Writing Option. I can still remember [the committee's] composition: Leonard [Rubinstein], [the poet] John Balaban, [fiction writer] Phil Klass, Doug Park, Jim Holahan, Judd Arnold, and myself. [. . .] It was a horrible experience for me, from which I had a three-month vacation teaching at the Iowa Workshop from October to December. [. . .] By the time I returned to sit in on meetings, the committee was at work on a gigantic 128-credit-hour major with tentacles in half a dozen different departments. A super Writing Option, [. . .] it came up for departmental discussion during Bob's last year as Head [1978–79] and was voted down.
>
> Of course I was a friend of Wilma's from before her arrival, and grew to like and admire her more and more during the years she spent [at Penn State]. But her agenda and mine were totally different. [. . .] The Writing Option had the students in the early '70s and a considerable faculty, and in my judgment the Writing Option with its peculiar ideology acted as a key opponent trying to block the path on which Wilma was set. [. . .] The way in which Wilma was redefining the teaching of writing held implications that went way beyond freshman comp and clashed fundamentally with Writing Option principles. (personal correspondence)

For Tom Rogers and for others, the revisions in the composition program at Penn State in 1977 meant the demise of principles that had guided writing instruction at the university for years: an engagement with literature; the formulation of the writing classroom as writing workshop; the employment of practicing and professional writers (not academics) as writing teachers; and the writing program as university department. What happened to composition in 1977 may have been for the better, but it affected other, related enterprises for the worse.

And on that note of conflict we close. History is like that.

Notes

Notes to Chapter 1

[1] See, for example, Campbell, Simmons, Bartholomae, and Hollis.

[2] Other recent overviews have attended to earlier eras, such as John Brereton's *Origins*, Nan Johnson's *Nineteenth-Century Rhetoric in North America*, Gregory Clark and Michael Halloran's *Oratorical Culture in Nineteenth-Century America*, and Thomas Miller's *The Formation of College English.*

[3] As our terminology and our commentary suggest, our approach to historiography has been shaped by Berlin, Crowley, Varnum, Harris, and the contributors to Vitanza's *Writing Histories* and Poulakos's *Rethinking the History of Rhetoric.* We have been especially attentive to Lester Faigley's call in "Veterans' Stories" for historical accounts that balance personal narratives and individual memories with hard archival and statistical data.

[4] In Burkean terms, our analytical method emphasizes the scene/act and scene/agent ratios, but it is not inattentive to other ratios as well.

[5] In a small way our study also exists in a tradition of elaborate studies of particular years, as in books like Breon-Guerry's famous *L'annee 1913,* Heller and Rudnick's *1915: The Cultural Moment,* Gallop's *Around 1981,* and North's *Reading 1922.*

Notes to Chapter 2

[6] When the Bakke case was finally decided in 1978, the controversy hardly ceased because the Court ruled very narrowly—in effect acknowledging that Mr. Bakke had been inappropriately denied admission but simultaneously ruling that affirmative action was nevertheless constitutional when pursued according to certain guidelines.

[7] Education-related publications discussed both the success and the struggles of these underrepresented groups to make their presence felt in higher education. The *Journal of Higher Education,* for example, outlined "Organizational Positions on Title IX: Conflicting Perspectives on Sex Discrimination in Education" (Fishel) and offered an overview of "Affirmative Action and Academic Hiring: A Case Study of a Value Conflict" (Steele and Green).

[8] *The Educational Record,* for example, discussed the intricacies of various discrimination suits brought against universities in the early to mid 1970s as a result of the "Growing Influence of Federal Regulations" (Solomon). The Pennsylvania State Board of Education explained that during the 1970s "such civil suits involving higher education have increased by 87 percent in federal courts" (11). Several highly controversial cases, including *De Funis v. Odegaard* (1974) at the University of Washington and the suit brought against the University of California by medical school student Alan Bakke (1978), carried cries of "reverse discrimination" into the headlines of national education news.

[9] While community colleges and two-year institutions provided a pool of potential transfer students, they also challenged the business of four-year institutions. The community colleges not only grew in size as a result of attracting new college students, they also grew by attracting students away from four-year institutions, perhaps reflecting emerging questions about the value of a four-year degree. In 1975 alone, the Pennsylvania Department of Education noted that over 1100 students transferred from four-year institutions to community colleges (Pennsylvania Dept. of Education 7).

Notes to Chapter 3

[10] Tenure-track vacancies in rhetoric and composition, creative writing, and linguistics dominated the MLA *Job Information List* by 1978, accounting for 57 percent of all tenure-track jobs listed in the *JIL* (Neel and Nelson 52).

[11] According to its annual program issue, MLA in 1977 offered five sessions on "computer-assisted instruction and research," a couple on technical writing, several on enrollment-driven curricular proposals, and a half dozen on one or another aspect of the job crisis. Propitiously enough, as people went off to those computer-related sessions at MLA in 1977, a graduate student at the University of Texas named Hugh Burns was in a basement office in Austin, working with computers himself (see sidebar).

[12] We gauged the reactions to "Why Johnny Can't Write" by examining the letters-to-the-editor sections of *Newsweek* and the *English Journal* as well as the October, 1977 edition of *Educational Digest* and miscellaneous other sources. One letter in *Newsweek* (January 5, 1976) was written by Elisabeth McPherson, whose work with students had been featured in the original "Why Johnny Can't Write" article: "Because learning to write is indeed learning to think," she wrote, "we put our emphasis on the thinking, not on the superficial etiquette involved in getting thoughts onto paper" (4). The November, 1976 issue of *English Journal* included such articles as "Why *Newsweek* Can't Tell Us Why Johnny Can't Write" (by Suzette Haden Elgin), and a feature close-up on "Why Can't Johnny and Jane Write?" that included articles by Timothy J. Bergen, Jr., Patricia Fox, Don Stoen, and Leslie Meskin and Robert P. Parker, Jr.; together the essays called for more writing in composition classes, different types of writing for different purposes, and a greater emphasis on process pedagogy.

Notes to Chapter 4

[13] According to Donald Stewart ("Composition Textbooks" 171), Young borrowed the term "current-traditional" from Daniel Fogarty (*Roots* 118) and delivered his essay on the topic first at a 1975 Buffalo Conference on the Composing Process.

[14] Current traditionalism is discussed at some length in Crowley, *Methodical Memory* and *Composition* (especially 94–95); and in Winterowd, *The English Department,* 89. The term has held pejorative connotations at least since it was discussed by Berlin (36–43), but subscribers to current traditional assumptions in the 1970s obviously regarded it as a thoroughly responsible approach and used it to accommodate a heterogeneous range of particular pedagogical practices.

[15] As Janet Emig pointed out at the beginning of the decade in her review of prior research on the composing process, study of school-age writers was both scant and unsystematic in 1971. By the beginning of the next decade, everything had changed; Maxine Hairston, surveying the field of composition in 1982, looked back to Emig, Britton, Flower and Hayes, and other cognitivist researchers as leaders in the "triumph of the process movement" in the 1970s, a triumph which had already revolutionized the field (see Faigley, *Fragments* 28-29). For a survey and critique of accounts of the process movement, see Ede's *Situating,* Part 2.

[16] Linda S. Flower and John R. Hayes, "Problem-Solving Strategies," 449n. The authors particularly note three diverse textbooks, each of which approaches the writing process usefully but differently: Young, Becker, and Pike's *Rhetoric: Discovery and Change* (1970), Peter Elbow's *Writing without Teachers* (1973), and William Coles's *Composing: Writing a Self-Creating Pro-*

cess (1974). Flower and Hayes and other researchers on composing were also aware of the work that had been done in England on composing by James Britton and his colleagues.

[17] Young moved to Carnegie Mellon in 1978.

[18] Richard Young in an informal personal conversation with one of us at the Rhetoric Society of America conference (June 6, 1998) noted that many people had remarked on his indebtedness to Kenneth Burke, but that his real debt was to Dewey, particularly in the area of problem definition.

[19] See, for example, W. Ross Winterowd, "The Grammar of Coherence" and Joseph Williams, who was trying to move linguistics beyond the sentence (i.e., into "non-linguistic linguistics" that would take into account things like genre, form, intention, situation, and even readers) in works like "Non-Linguistic Linguistics and the Teaching of Style." Because the account that follows is focused on the 1970s, we are less attentive to work in linguistics by influential earlier figures such as C. C. Fries, Edward Sapir, and Porter Perrin.

[20] In fact, Chomsky himself renounced all efforts to adapt his theory to pedagogy, or even to usage; see Luthy (1977). Incidentally, the notion of kernel sentences was in Chomsky's 1957 *Syntactic Structures,* but he dropped the idea in his 1965 *Aspects of the Theory of Syntax.*

[21] For a somewhat different and more complete history of sentence-based pedagogies of the 1970s, see Connors, "Erasure." Connors includes a discussion of sentence imitation exercises, a practice that influenced textbooks written by sentence combiners.

[22] Critics of sentence combining sometimes resisted as well the hyperbolic claim of proponents that sentence combining improved writing "without grammar instruction" when what the sentence-combiners really meant was "without traditional grammar instruction." The best scholarly overview of sentence combining and its roots is Kerek, Daiker, and Morenberg's monograph in *Perceptual and Motor Skills* (1980); see also Connors, "Erasure." For a criticism of sentence combining that summarized contemporary misgivings, see two papers at a 1978 conference on the subject: Elbow's "The Challenge for Sentence Combining," and Hake and Williams's "Sentence Expanding."

[23] That Christensen used the word "generative" was coincidental: he did not derive the term from the new linguistics.

[24] For a fuller personal history of the "Students' Right to Their Own Language" episode, see Smitherman, "CCCC's Role."

[25] Some have called Shaughnessy insensitive to difference, an "accommodationist" who assumed the superiority of standard English and who betrayed a relative intolerance toward border languages and dialects. For a patient and informed discussion of those charges, see Gray-Rosendale.

[26] Lunsford's fellow graduate students John Ruszkiewicz, Betsy Brown, Mary Rosner, and Carmen Schmersahl, who had all taught the pilot basic writing course at Ohio State in 1975–76, spread the gospel when they earned positions at the University of Texas, Penn State, The University of Louisville, and Mt. St. Mary's College. Frank O'Hare joined the faculty at Ohio State in 1978, succeeding Miller as director of composition.

[27] For a convenient short history of writing centers, see Boquet.

[28] For more information on the state of technical writing instruction before the 1970s, including information on the explosion of interest in the subject, begin with Souther.

[29] Summer seminars for scientists, engineers, and teachers of professional writing had been offered at Michigan by W. Earl Britton from the early 1960s. Mathes and Stevenson took an elaborate and successful program and changed the emphasis (Young, personal correspondence). For an account of the early years of ATTW, see Cunningham, "The Founding"; for the birth of CPTSC, see Pearsall and Warren.

[30] Francis Christensen's *Notes toward a New Rhetoric* in its title echoes the link between linguistics and "the new rhetoric." Actually, a term like "renewed rhetoric" might be better than "new rhetoric," since as we will see, so many of the new rhetorics had affiliations of one kind or another with classical rhetoric.

[31] One of us has turned up correspondence between Burke and Winterowd that dates from the years when Winterowd was teaching in Montana and that is now on deposit in the Kenneth Burke Papers at Penn State.

[32] Burke's relation to the Chicago School was always an uneasy and complicated one, however, with influences running in both directions. Burke, for example, felt that Richard Weaver borrowed from his work far more than Weaver acknowledged, and Booth in *Critical Understanding* documents his own somewhat vexed interchanges with Burke. Burke's relationship with Richard McKeon began when both were students at Columbia before 1920 (Selzer, *Kenneth Burke*). McKeon invited Burke to teach at Chicago during the summer of 1938, and Burke returned on several other occasions. James Sledd (personal interview) recalls that Burke led a seminar at Chicago in 1950 that was attended by Sledd, Weaver, Wilma Ebbitt, and possibly Booth and others; Sledd also recalls that he shared an office with Elder Olson, who introduced Sledd to the rhetoric of Whately!).

[33] R. D. Walshe criticized Booth's version of rhetorical stance in a 1977 article and proposed how it could be accommodated to process pedagogy.

[34] On the tension between New Criticism and the Chicago critics, see the Chicago School "manifesto" *Critics and Criticism: Ancient and Modern,* edited by R. S. Crane in 1952, a book that contained essays by Crane, McKeon, Elder Olson, Norman Maclean and others. As we have noted, New Criticism continued throughout the 1950s and even the 1960s and 1970s despite

the telling attack of the Chicago School, but when prestige of the New Criticism plummeted in the 1970s, support for the Chicago School and for its second-generation hero Booth proportionally soared (e.g., the Chicago School journal *Critical Inquiry*, begun in 1974, was by 1977 the hottest journal for work in critical theory)—not least because Booth's learned, clear prose found a broader audience than had the more turgid prose of the people collected in *Critics and Criticism*. For a detailed summary and history of the Chicago School, see Leitch; McKeon; and Booth, "Between Two Generations." For information about Booth's influence, see Antczak.

[35] Weaver, Wilma Ebbitt, and James Sledd taught undergraduates in the College at Chicago, while McKeon, Crane, and Olson were involved mainly with Division matters at Chicago pertaining to graduate studies.

[36] The 1977–78 WPA board included Harvey Wiener, Win Horner, Joseph Comprone, Lawrence Kasden, Ken Bruffee, David Bartholomae, Harry Crosby, James Raymond, Elaine Maimon, and Richard Raspa. In our interview with Harvey Wiener, he placed the date of the original MLA meeting in December, 1977, but it is clear from other sources that it was 1976. For help in confirming the date, we thank Susan McLeod, who also learned from Wiener that WPA got up and running so quickly during 1977 because it capitalized on a prior organization in New York known as CAWS—the CUNY Association of Writing Supervisors. See also Heckathorn.

[37] Frank D'Angelo recalls that Texas Woman's University under the auspices of the Federation of North Texas Universities sponsored symposia on rhetoric in the mid-1970s that included Edward Corbett, Gary Tate, Winston Weathers, Kenneth Burke, Wilbur Samuel Howell, Ross Winterowd, Richard Larson, Thomas Sloane, and many others ("Professing" 271).

Notes to Chapter 5

[38] The lack of funding led to a deduction in services for, among other things, the University Park library in October of 1977. Students protested this cutback, staging a "study-in" and occupying the library over the nights of October 11 and 12.

[39] If the paper shortage hampered the teaching practices of composition instructors, it also influenced their responses to student writing. Freshman composition papers preserved from one 1978 section contain several comments encouraging students not to skip lines in their drafts because such a practice uses too much paper. The revision process might be easier with more space to write drafts, but the economics of paper scarcity had to be reckoned with as well.

[40] Interestingly, two colleges that would significantly increase their enrollments in the late 1970s and 1980—Business and Engineering—also lost

over 20 percent of their students (relative to university enrollments) from 1969–1977.

[41] Rubinstein, "Let Us Teach Writing as a Subject." See also an unsigned article in the *Daily Collegian,* October 8, 1976. Not all Writing Option faculty agreed with the proposal. Peter Schneeman, for example, believed that the plan would simply be a reversion to the pre-1960 era—when composition and literature had existed independently of one another at Penn State. And the Dean of Liberal Arts did not appreciate that the plan was submitted not just to him but to the news media (Frank, personal interview).

[42] In 1971, the Association of Pennsylvania State University Branch Campus Faculty Members filed a petition with the Pennsylvania Labor Relations Board to represent the faculty, librarians, and counselors of the Commonwealth Campuses, claiming that "the 18 campuses had an identifiable community of interests which was separate and distinct from faculty at the University Park campus" (Greshenfeld and Mortimer 206). University administrators at University Park opposed such a proposal on the grounds that it would fragment the university and interfere with teaching and research progress on a university-wide level. After a series of nine hearings on the Commonwealth Campuses' petition to organize separately for collective bargaining, the PLRB dismissed the petition on the basis that the Commonwealth Campus faculty "did not constitute an appropriate bargaining unit" (206).

[43] Much of the concern about remediation arose not from the situation at University Park but from the situation on Commonwealth Campuses, where many more students were identified as deficient in math and writing. In 1977, for example, 413 students in math and 307 students in English were identified as requiring remediation at University Park. The totals for other campuses, however, were much higher, with 781 Commonwealth Campus students in math and 759 in writing not meeting minimum standards of performance (Joint Commission, "Legislative" Appendix F). The *Harrisburg Evening News* reported in March of 1978 that 51 percent of the associate degree candidates tested at all Penn State Campuses were found deficient in English or math ("PSU Teaching").

Notes to Chapter 6

[44] A sixth edition, prepared with her husband David Ebbitt, appeared in 1978.

[45] The original English 3 ran through the spring term of 1975, when the revised course came into existence. However, the revised course continued under the name English 3 until fall 1977, when its name became English 20.

[46] The following statement reflects the connections between the first and second courses; a similar statement can be found in every syllabus from fall 1975 onward: "This syllabus tries to carry out, as far as it is possible, the idea that English 10 (English 1) and English 20 (English 3) form one program in composition and rhetoric. The assignments in analysis and argument described here depend heavily on the skills of organization and development that students practice in English 10; but in their scope and complexity the assignments come closer than those of English 10 to the reports, memos, briefs, and proposals that students will write in their college courses and in their professions. [. . .] English 20 must not only progress logically from English 10 but must also have its own beginning, middle, and end; it must not only be more challenging, but must also be able to cover again the ground that any composition course must cover" ("Preface," *English 20 Teaching Packet*). The statement echoes sentiments in the Freshman English Committee recommendations summarized by Wilma Ebbitt in her memo to Arthur Lewis, May 12, 1975.

[47] Three items, available in the department's Resource Room, were suggested as "further reading" for instructors: Janet Emig, *The Composing Process of Twelfth Graders;* John Warnock, "New Rhetoric and the Grammar of Pedagogy"; and Roger Garrison, "One-to-One: Tutorial Instruction in Freshman Composition." Though instructors apparently were not required to read this material, even the suggestion that they might do so reveals the composition program's increasing awareness of the utility of the growing body of research and theory for rank-and-file instructors, and not just those charged with curricular design.

[48] The student papers quoted here were preserved within a faculty member's files from the 1977-1978 academic year. Because they were not originally collected with the intent of publication, student permission to excerpt them was not secured at the time of collection. As a result, we have elected to omit attribution to specific student writers in this text.

[49] At the time, Penn State worked under an unusual "term calendar" which permitted students to complete a semester-long three-credit course in ten weeks. A three-credit course in composition, for example, typically met for 4.5 hours per week for a total of 45 classroom contact hours, and students typically limited themselves to three or four such intensive courses per term. The system, designed to permit students to complete degrees in three years if they wished to study year round and intended to lead to more fully enrolled summer terms and a more intensive use of facilities in the summer, was discarded in the early 1980s.

[50] Just how much Penn State's program was developing on the model of the University of Chicago is apparent from a reading of Henry Sams's chapter "Writing," his contribution to "An Account of the College of the University of Chicago, by present and former members of the faculty," published as

The Idea and Practice of General Education. Chicago's program was organized around courses in exposition, argument, and style. There was also what we would today call a "basic writing" course, known at Chicago as "English Deficiency (Writing)."

[51] English 30 demands little of our attention in this essay because only a very few sections of Honors Composition and Rhetoric were offered in the mid-1970s and because it occupied little of the department's intellectual and ideological energy. Originally numbered English 2, it was an alternative to English 3/20 for students who were placed there and who consequently were exempted from English 10. Until it gained more prominence in the 1980s, the course was essentially designed by its individual instructors, mostly as a more sophisticated version of Leonard Rubinstein's English 3. Professor Ebbitt, however, did retain an interest in keeping as much imaginative literature as possible out of English 30.

[52] On the topic of basic writing throughout the Penn State System, Wiener stated, "I don't think the problem was at all profound at [the University Park campus of] Penn State. [. . .] It was essentially for the branch campuses" (personal interview). Kolln agreed, saying that "one of the things about our remedial program was that we did incorporate all of the campuses in truth because of course most of the freshmen [who need basic writing] are at the branch campuses." When asked how the other campuses reacted to the new syllabus, Kolln was realistic: "I think we've always sort of acted as though we knew best at University Park and handed it down" (personal interview). There was no way of knowing whether or not the syllabus was being followed, but because basic writing was more of an issue on the Commonwealth Campuses it can be assumed that Wiener's suggestions were of some use to them. Indeed, in the "Basic Writing Instructor's Resource Book," Wiener emphasized the following intentions: "Our hope is that the ideas [contained in this syllabus] will lead to better ones, that the suggestions will stimulate thinking about the problems of the basic writer, and that classroom experience growing out of these ideas will uncover new and productive possibilities in research" (I: 4). Though intended to "standardize instruction throughout the state," the syllabus Wiener designed was also presented openly, "in the spirit of scholarship" ("Basic Writing" 1).

[53] Frank, on the other hand, recalls the incident not as his effort to contain Wiener but as a collegial attempt to advise Wiener on politic ways of proceeding (personal interview).

[54] Instructors at the Commonwealth Campuses, inundated with basic writers, understandably balked at flunking students on the basis of one exam, which essentially disregarded an entire semester of work. Teachers at some campuses passed students regardless of whether they had "eight errors or four," but University Park stuck strictly to the standards set out by the basic writing program. Frank recalls that Snyder was a major figure in the

reform of basic skills instruction at Penn State. The department "really had to please her," and he attended many meetings and wrote many memos to respond to her concerns (Frank, personal interview).

[55] The Committee also created a tracking system that followed students' progress: if they reached their third semester without "removing their deficiency," students were removed from degree status. This device was intended to keep students moving through the system, but it proved to be too expensive and was dropped by 1980.

[56] Special thanks to Ronald Maxwell and Nancy Lowe for the use of their extensive personal archives related to this issue.

[57] Not everyone remembers the staff meetings so fondly. "You refer to the 'famous staff meetings' at Chicago [and Penn State] that Wilma [Ebbitt] was involved in," remembers Tom Rogers. "What was so famous about those meetings? Famous to whom? Famous for what? The meetings I attended alternately bored or drove me crazy, though Phil Roth [the novelist] and I had a lot of fun making jokes about them. [. . .] Phil used those staff meetings in *Letting Go,* his first novel. Is that what made them famous? Maybe they were better before my time, though many of the old war horses were still around when I was teaching comp at Chicago. I thought Richard "Ideas Have Consequences" Weaver was a colossal dud" (personal correspondence).

[58] Consistent with that point of view, Rubinstein remarked negatively on the professional language used in the introduction to this essay when he was asked to comment on a draft. Today he thinks of rhetoric as too academic to be relevant to the teaching of writing: "Rhetoric was created when enrollment in literature dropped dramatically throughout the country. Teachers of literature needed a job, and by creating the area of rhetoric, a need was satisfied. But its creation also created a vocabulary in writing that was incomprehensible to the average college student. It was the language of PhD candidates" (personal interview).

[59] The third edition of *Reporting Technical Information* offered a substantial opening section entitled "The Process of Technical Reporting" and included chapters on invention, audience analysis, arrangement, and revision.

Sources Consulted and Cited

Interviews

Arnold, Judd. Personal interview. 8 Apr. 1998.
Fahnestock, Jeanne. Personal interview. 4 Apr. 1998.
Frank, Robert Worth III. Personal interview. 9 Aug. 1999.
Greenfield, Diane. Personal interview. Sept. 13, 1999.
Lunsford, Andrea. Personal interview. 16 Sept. 1998.
Knapp, Edgar. Personal interview. 25 Mar. 1998.
Kolln, Martha. Personal interview. 16 Mar. 1998.
Lowe, Nancy. Personal interview. 23 Mar. 1998.
Maxwell, Ron. Personal interview. 25 Mar. 1998.
Moore, John. Personal interview. 22 Apr. 1998.
Rubinstein, S. Leonard. Personal interviews. 8 Apr. 1998; 19 July 1999.
Schneeman, Peter. Personal interview. 23 Mar. 1998.
Secor, Marie. Personal interview. 4 Apr. 1998.
Sledd, James. Personal interview. 5 July 1999.
Wiener, Harvey. Personal interview. 3 Apr. 1998.

Unpublished and Local Documents

Bailey, Stephen. "Needed Changes in Liberal Education." Liberal Arts Steering Committee, eds. 4–12.

Coelen, Stephen. "What are the Anticipated Career Opportunities for LA Graduate Students?" Liberal Arts Steering Committee, eds. 35–41.

Coles, William. "Letter to Dr. Dorothy Wartenberg." Division of Fellowships, National Endowment for the Humanities. 4 Sept. 1979.

DuBois, Charles C. "6 Offer Plan to Improve Student Writing Skills." *Centre Daily Times* 5 Nov. 1976: 19.

"Ebbitt Fellowship Will Aid Graduate Students." *Rhetor Rooter: The Penn State Composition Program Newsletter* May 1993: 1.

Ebbitt, Wilma. "Memo to Arthur O. Lewis et al on English 3 Review." 12 May 1975.

Ebbitt, Wilma, and Doug Park. "Memo to English 3 Staff." 22 May 1975.

English 10 Teaching Packet. Dept. of English. University Park, PA: Pennsylvania State University, Aug. 1977.

English 20 Teaching Packet. Dept. of English. University Park, PA: Pennsylvania State University, Aug. 1977.

Enos, Richard. Email to Jack Selzer. 7 Jan. 2000.

Frank, Robert. "Point of View [Interview]." *Intercom* 13 Jan. 1977: 2–3.

Freshman English Committee. *English 1 and 3: Fall 1975 Syllabus Packet.* Dept. of English. University Park, PA: Pennsylvania State University, 1975.

—. *English 3 Sourcebook: Fall 1976.* Dept. of English. University Park, PA: Pennsylvania State University, 1976.

—. "Proposal for Revised English 1 and English 3." Dept. of English, Pennsylvania State University. 20 May 1975.

Gregg, Richard. "The Student of the 1980's." Liberal Arts Steering Committee, eds. 12–20.

Greshenfeld, Walter, and Kenneth P. Mortimer. *Faculty Collective Bargaining Activity in Pennsylvania, the First Five Years (1970–1975). A Report to the Carnegie Corporation of New York of a Statewide Study.* Philadelphia: Center for Labor and Manpower Studies, Temple University, 1976.

Joint Presidential-Senate Commission to Study Remedial Education. "Legislative Report to the President and the University Faculty Senate." 1 Feb. 1977.

Joint Presidential-Senate Commission to Study Remedial Education, Helen Snyder, Coordinator. "Basic Skills Program for Lower Division Students at the Pennsylvania State University 1977–1980: An Experimental Program." 23 May 1977.

Kolln, Martha. Memo to composition fac. 15 Dec. 1978.

Lauer, Janice. Personal correspondence. 11 Aug. 2005.

Liberal Arts Steering Committee, eds. *The College of the Liberal Arts in the 1980's.* Proceedings of the Faculty Conference of the College of the Liberal Arts, University Park, PA., Spring 1977. University Park, PA: Pennsylvania State University, 1978.

Lindemann, Erika, and Gary Tate. "Joint Evaluation Report of Pennsylvania State University's Freshman English Program." Report submitted to Liberal Arts Dean Stanley Paulson, Pennsylvania State University, University Park, PA. 7 Oct. 1977.

McLeod, Susan. Personal correspondence. 7 Mar. 2001.

MET Liberation Army. "To All MET Freaks." Dept. of English, Pennsylvania State University, University Park, PA. 15 July 1974.

O'Donnell, William. Memo to English dept. fac. 8 Jan. 1979.

Oswald, John. "The Pennsylvania State University 1976–1977 State Appropriations Request." Statement submitted to The Appropriation Committees, Pennsylvania State Senate, 25 Feb. 1976, and Pennsylvania State

House of Representatives, 1 Mar. 1976. University Park, PA: Pennsylvania State University, 1976.

Park, Douglas. Memo to Instructors of English 3. Dept. of English, Pennsylvania State University, University Park, PA. 1 Mar. 1977.

—. Email to Wendy Sharer. 14 Jan. 1999.

Park, Douglas, and Edward Uehling, eds. *The Penn State Reader: 20.* University Park, PA: Pennsylvania State University, 1977.

Paulson, Stanley G. "Liberal Arts: Future Tense or Tense Future?" Liberal Arts Steering Committee, eds. 1–3.

Pennsylvania Dept. of Education. *An Analysis of Student Transfers from Pennsylvania Community Colleges.* Harrisburg, PA: Pennsylvania Dept. of Education, 1976.

Pennsylvania Division of Educational Statistics. Pennsylvania Dept. of Education. *Fall College Enrollments by Racial/Ethnic Categories in Pennsylvania 1978.* Harrisburg, PA: Pennsylvania Dept. of Education, 1979.

Pennsylvania Economy League, State Division. *Higher Education and the Economy: A Survey of the Impacts on Pennsylvania's Economy of Its Colleges and Universities, the Statewide Impacts.* 1981.

Pennsylvania State Board of Education. *The Master Plan for Higher Education in Pennsylvania, 1978.* Harrisburg, PA: The Board, 1979.

Pennsylvania State University. "1976–77 Appropriation Request." 25 Feb. 1976.

"Policy Governing the Freshman Writing Program." Dept. of English, Pennsylvania State University, University Park, PA. 2 Oct. 1969.

"PSU Teaching What Secondary Schools Failed to: Basic Writing." *Harrisburg Evening News* 28 Mar. 1978. C4.

Rogers, Thomas. Personal correspondence. 23 Jan. 2000.

Rubinstein, S. Leonard. "New Approaches to English 3." *Faculty Bulletin* 27 Aug. 1965. 3.

Senate Special Committee on Basic Skills. "Legislative Report to the President of the Faculty Senate." Pennsylvania State University, University Park, PA. 1 Feb. 1977.

Senate Special Committee on Basic Skills. "Basic Skills Program (Informational Report)." Pennsylvania State University, University Park, PA. 6 Dec. 1977.

Sledd, James. Personal correspondence. 5 Feb. 2000; 9 Mar. 2000.

Unsigned article. *The Daily Collegian,* 14 Dec. 1977.

Warnock, Tilly. Personal correspondence. 31 Jan. 2000.

Wiener, Harvey. "Basic Writing Instructor's Resource Book." Dept. of English, Pennsylvania State University, University Park, PA. 1976.

Young, Richard. Personal correspondence. 14 Aug. 2000.

Secondary Sources

Alm, Kent G., Elwood B. Ehrle, and Bill R. Webster. “Managing Faculty Reductions” *Journal of Higher Education* 48.2 (Mar.-Apr. 1977): 153–63.

Almagno, Stephanie A. “An NEH Fellowship Examined: Social Networks and Composition History.” Diss. University of Rhode Island, 1994.

AWP Catalogue of Writing Programs. 3rd ed. Norfolk, VA: AWP, 1980.

Antczak, Frederick J. *Rhetoric and Pluralism: Legacies of Wayne Booth.* Columbus, OH: Ohio State UP, 1995.

Austin, J. A. *How to Do Things with Words.* Cambridge: Harvard UP, 1975.

Bailey, Stephen K. “Needed Changes in Liberal Education.” *Educational Record.* 58.3 (Summer 1977): 250–58.

Barthes, Roland. *Image—Music—Text.* Trans. Stephen Heath. New York: Hill and Wang, 1977.

Bartholomae, David. “Afterword: Around 1980.” *Pre/Text: The First Decade.* Ed. Victor Vitanza. Pittsburgh: U of Pittsburgh P, 1993. 287–98.

Beck, Paula, Thom Hawkins, and Marcia Silver. “Peer Tutoring at a Community College: Training and Using Peer Tutors.” *College English* 40 (1978): 437–49.

Bergen, Timothy L. “Why Can't Johnny Write?” *English Journal* 65.8 (1976): 36–7.

Berlin, James. *Rhetoric and Reality: Writing Instruction in American Colleges, 1900–1985.* Carbondale: Southern Illinois UP, 1987.

Berlin, James, and Robert P. Inkster. “Current-Traditional Rhetoric: Paradigm and Practice.” *Freshman English News* 8.3 (1980): 1–4, 13–14.

Bezilla, Michael. *Penn State: An Illustrated History.* University Park: Penn State UP, 1985. 2 September 2007 <http://www.libraries.psu.edu/speccolls/psua/psgeneralhistory/bezillapshistory/083s14.htm>.

Berthoff, Ann E. *The Making of Meaning.* Montclair, NJ: Boynton-Cook, 1981.

Bilsky, Manuel, McCrea Hazlitt, Robert Streeter, and Richard Weaver. “Looking for an Argument.” *College English* 14 (1953): 210–16.

Bitzer, Lloyd, and Edwin Black, eds. *The Prospect of Rhetoric: A Report of the National Development Project, Sponsored by Speech Communication Association.* Englewood Cliffs: Prentice Hall, 1971.

Boquet, Elizabeth H. “‘Our Little Secret’: A History of Writing Centers, Pre- to Post-Open Admissions.” *College Composition and Communication* 50 (1999): 463–82.

Booth, Wayne. “Between Two Generations: The Heritage of the Chicago School.” *Profession 82.* Ed. Richard Brod and Phyllis Franklin. New York: MLA, 1982. 20–26.

—. *Critical Understanding: The Powers and Limits of Pluralism.* Chicago: U of Chicago P, 1979.

—. “The Revival of Rhetoric.” Steinmann 1–15.

—. *The Rhetoric of Fiction.* Chicago: U of Chicago P, 1961.

—. "The Rhetorical Stance." *College Composition and Communication* 14 (1963): 139–45.

Bradshaw, Jon. "Elvis: A Dossier." *Esquire* October 1977: 96–97.

Breon-Guerry, Liliane. *L'annee 1913.* Paris: Klincksieck, 1971.

Brereton, John. *The Origins of Composition Studies in the American College, 1875–1925: A Documentary History.* Pittsburgh: U of Pittsburgh P, 1994.

Britton, W. Earl. "What Is Technical Writing?" *College Composition and Communication* 14 (1965): 113–16.

Britton, James. *Language and Learning.* New York: Penguin, 1977.

Britton, James, et al. *The Development of Writing Abilities (11–18), A Report.* London: Macmillan; and Urbana, NCTE, 1975.

Brooks, Cleanth, and Robert Penn Warren, eds. *Understanding Poetry: An Anthology for College Students.* New York: H. Holt, 1938.

Brubacher, John S., and Willis Rudy. *Higher Education in Transition: A History of American Colleges and Universities.* 4th ed. New Brunswick, NJ: Transaction Publishers, 1997.

Burke, Kenneth. *Counter-Statement.* Berkeley: U of California P, 1968.

—. *A Grammar of Motives.* New York: G. Braziller, 1955.

—. *The Philosophy of Literary Form.* Berkeley: U of California P, 1974.

—. "Questions and Answers about the Pentad." *College Composition and Communication* 29 (1978): 330–35.

—. *A Rhetoric of Motives.* Berkeley: U of California P, 1969.

Campbell, JoAnn. "Controlling Voices: The Legacy of English A at Radcliffe College 1883–1917." *College Composition and Communication* 43 (1992): 472–85.

Carter, Jimmy. "The President's Proposed Energy Policy." 18 April 1977. *Vital Speeches of the Day.* 43.14 (May 1977): 418-20.

Chomsky, Noam. *Syntactic Structures.* The Hague: Mouton, 1957.

—. *Topics in the Theory of Generative Grammar.* The Hague: Mouton, 1966.

—. *Aspects of the Theory of Syntax.* The Hague: Mouton, 1965.

Christensen, Francis. *Notes toward a New Rhetoric.* New York: Harper, 1976.

Clark, Gregory, and Michael Halloran, eds. *Oratorical Culture in Nineteenth-Century America: Transformations in the Theory and Practice of Rhetoric.* Carbondale: Southern Illinois UP, 1993.

Coles, William. *Composing: Writing as a Self-Creating Process.* Rochelle Park, NJ: Hayden, 1974.

—. *The Plural I: The Teaching of Writing.* New York: Holt, Rinehart and Winston, 1978.

Comprone, Joseph. "Kenneth Burke and the Teaching of Writing." *College Composition and Communication* 29 (1978): 336–40.

Connors, Robert. *Composition-Rhetoric: Backgrounds, Theory, and Pedagogy.* Pittsburgh: U of Pittsburgh P, 1997.

—. "The Erasure of the Sentence." *College Composition and Communication* 52 (2000): 96–126.

—. "The Rise and Fall of the Modes of Discourse." *College Composition and Communication* 32 (1981): 444–63.

—. "The Rise of Technical Communication in America." *Journal of Technical Writing and Communication* 12 (1982): 329–52.

Cooper, Charles R., and Lee Odell, eds. *Evaluating Writing: Describing, Measuring, Judging.* Urbana: NCTE, 1977.

Corbett, Edward P. J. *Classical Rhetoric for the Modern Student.* 2nd ed. Oxford: Oxford UP, 1971.

—. "How I Became a Teacher of Composition." Roen, Brown, and Enos 1–6.

Crane, R. S., ed. *Critics and Criticism: Ancient and Modern.* Chicago: U of Chicago P, 1952.

Crowley, Sharon. "Around 1971: Current-Traditional Rhetoric and Process Models of Composing." *Composition in the Twenty-First Century: Crisis and Change.* Ed. Lynn Bloom et al. Carbondale: Southern Illinois UP, 1996. 64–74.

—. *Composition in the University: Historical and Polemical Essays.* Pittsburgh: U of Pittsburgh P, 1998.

—. "Linguistics and Composition Instruction 1950–1980." *Written Communication* 6 (1989): 480–505.

—. *The Methodical Memory: Invention in Current-Traditional Rhetoric.* Carbondale: Southern Illinois UP, 1990.

—. "Of Gorgias and Grammatology." *College Composition and Communication* 30 (1979): 279–84.

—. "Response to Edward M. White." *Journal of Basic Writing* 15 (1996): 88–91.

—. "When Ideology Motivates Theory: The Case of the Man from Weaverville." *Rhetoric Review* 20 (2001): 66–93.

Cunningham, Donald. "The Founding of the ATTW and Its Journal." *Technical Communication Quarterly* 13 (2004): 121–130.

Cunningham, Donald, and Herman Estrin, eds. *The Teaching of Technical Writing.* Urbana: NCTE, 1975.

Daiker, Donald, Max Morenberg, and Andrew Kerek. "Sentence Combining and Syntactic Maturity in Freshman English." *College Composition and Communication* 29 (1978): 36–41.

—. *The Writer's Options.* New York: Random House, 1978.

D'Angelo, Frank. *A Conceptual Theory of Rhetoric.* Cambridge, MA: Winthrop Publishers, 1975.

—. "The Freshman Composition Program at Arizona State University." Neel 46–51.

—. "Notes toward a Semantic Theory of Rhetoric within a Case Grammar Framework." *College Composition and Communication* 28 (1976): 359–62.

—. "In Search of the American Dream." Roen, Brown, and Enos. 55–64.

—. *Process and Thought in Composition.* Cambridge, MA: Winthrop Publishers, 1977.

—. "Professing Rhetoric and Composition." *History, Reflection, and Narrative: The Professionalization of Composition, 1963–83.* Ed. Mary Rosner, Beth Boehm, and Debra Journet. Stamford, CN: Ablex, 2000. 269–81.

Damerst, William. *Clear Technical Reports.* New York: Harcourt, 1972.

Daniels, Harvey, and Steven Zemelman. *A Writing Project: Training Teachers of Composition from Kindergarten to College.* Portsmouth: Heinemann, 1985.

Deskins, Donald R. "Winners and Losers: A Regional Assessment of Minority Enrollment and Earned Degrees in U.S. Colleges and Universities, 1974–84." *College in Black and White: African American Students in Predominantly White and in Historically Black Public Universities.* Ed. Walter R. Allen, Edgar G. Epps, and Nesha Z. Haniff. Albany: SUNY P, 1991. 17–40.

Dewey, John. *Democracy and Education.* New York: Macmillan, 1916.

—. *Logic: The Theory of Inquiry.* New York: H. Holt, 1938.

Eastman, Arthur M., ed. *The Norton Reader: An Anthology of Expository Prose.* New York: Norton, 1977.

Ebbitt, Wilma. "Richard Weaver: Teacher of Rhetoric." *Georgia Review* 17 (1963): 415–18.

Ebbitt, Wilma, and James Sledd. *Dictionaries and THAT Dictionary.* New York: Scott, 1962.

Ebbitt, Wilma, and Porter G. Perrin, eds. *Writer's Guide and Index to English.* 4th ed. New York: Scott, 1968.

—. *Writer's Guide and Index to English.* 5th ed. New York: Scott, 1972.

Ebbitt, Wilma, and Russel Nye. *Structures in Reading and Writing.* New York: Scott, 1961.

Ebbitt, Wilma, and William T. Lenehan. *The Writer's Reader.* New York: Scott, 1968.

Eberly, Rosa. "The Force of Wilma Ebbitt." Paper given at the Penn State Conference on Rhetoric and Composition: Rhetorical Education in America. State College, PA. 7 July 1999.

Eco, Umberto. *A Theory of Semiotics.* Bloomington: Indiana UP, 1976.

Eddy, Edward. "What Happened to Student Values?" *Educational Record* 58.1 (Winter 1977): 7–17.

Ede, Lisa. *Situating Composition: Composition Studies and the Politics of Location.* Carbondale: Southern Illinois UP, 2004.

Elbow, Peter. *Writing without Teachers.* New York: Oxford UP, 1973.

—. "The Challenge for Sentence Combining." Daiker, Kerek, and Morenberg 232–45.

Elgin, Richard. "Pennsylvania." *The Americana Annual: An Encyclopedia of Current Events 1977.* Chicago: Encyclopedia Americana, 392-97.

Elgin, Suzette Haden. "Why *Newsweek* Can't Tell Us Why Johnny Can't Write." *English Journal* 65.8 (1976): 29–35.

Emig, Janet. *The Composing Processes of Twelfth Graders.* Urbana: NCTE, 1971.

—. "Writing as a Mode of Learning." *College Composition and Communication* 28.1 (1977): 122–28.

Fahnestock, Jeanne, and Marie Secor. *A Rhetoric of Argument.* New York: Random House, 1982.

Faigley, Lester. *Fragments of Rationality: Postmodernity and the Subject of Composition.* Pittsburgh: U of Pittsburgh P, 1992.

—. "Veterans' Stories on the Porch." *History, Reflection, and Narrative: The Professionalization of Composition, 1963–83.* Ed. Mary Rosner, Beth Boehm, and Debra Journet. Stamford, CT: Ablex, 2000. 23–38.

Featherman, Sandra, and William T. Rosenberg. *Jews, Blacks, and Ethnics: The 1978 "Vote White" Charter Campaign in Philadelphia.* Philadelphia: Institute for Public Policy Studies, Temple University, 1979.

Fishel, Andrew. "Organizational Positions on Title IX: Conflicting Perspectives on Sex Discrimination in Education." *Journal of Higher Education* 47 (1976): 93–105.

Flower, Linda, and John R. Hayes. "The Cognition of Discovery: Defining a Rhetorical Problem." *College Composition and Communication* 31 (1980): 21–32.

—. "Problem-Solving Strategies and the Writing Process." *College English* 39 (1977): 449–61.

Flower, Linda. *Problem-Solving Strategies for Writing.* New York: Harcourt, 1981.

Fogarty, Daniel. *Roots for a New Rhetoric.* New York: Bureau of Publications, Teachers College, Columbia U, 1959.

Fox, Patricia. "Why Johnny Can't and Cat In the Hat: An Article in Two Parts." *English Journal* 65.8 (1976): 36–37.

Franklin, Phyllis. "From the Editor." *Profession 1997.* New York: MLA, 1997. 1–7.

Freed, Richard D., ed. *Eloquent Dissent: The Writings of James Sledd.* Portmouth, NH: Boynton/Cook, 1996.

Gallop, Jane. *Around 1981: Academic Feminist Literary Theory.* New York: Routledge, 1992.

Garrison, Roger. "One-to-One: Tutorial Instruction in Freshman Composition." *New Directions for Community Colleges* 2.1 (1974): 55–84.

Geckle, George. "The Dual Masters Degree" *ADE Bulletin: Special Issue on the State of the Discipline, 1970s-1980s* 62 (Sept.–Nov. 1979): 42–45.

Gere, Anne Ruggles. *Intimate Practices: Literacy and Cultural Work in U.S. Women's Clubs, 1880–1920.* Urbana: U of Illinois P, 1997.

Gibson, Walker. *Tough, Sweet, and Stuffy.* Bloomington: Indiana UP, 1966.

—. "Writing Programs and the Department of English." *ADE Bulletin* 61 (Feb. 1979): 19–22.

Gray-Rosendale, Laura. "Inessential Writings: Shaughnessy's Legacy in a Socially Constructed Landscape." *Journal of Basic Writing* 17 (1998): 43–75.

Gregg, Lee W., and Erwin R. Steinberg, eds. *Cognitive Processes in Writing.* Hillsdale, NJ: Erlbaum, 1980.

Griffin, C. Williams, ed. *Teaching Writing in All Disciplines.* San Francisco: Jossey-Bass, 1982.

Hairston, Maxine. "The Winds of Change: Thomas Kuhn and the Revolution in the Teaching of Writing." *College Composition and Communication* 33 (1982): 76–88.

Hake, Rosemary, and Joseph Williams. "Sentence Expanding: Not Can, or How, but When." *Sentence Combining and the Teaching of Writing.* Ed. Donald Daiker, Andrew Kerek, and Max Morenberg. Conway, AR: L&S Books, 1979. 134–46.

Halpern, Jeanne W., ed. *Teaching Business Writing: Approaches, Plans, Pedagogy, Research.* Urbana: American Business Communication Assoc., 1983.

Haraway, Donna. "Situated Knowledges: The Science Question in Feminism and the Privilege of Partial Perspective." *Feminist Studies* 14 (1988): 575–99.

Harris, Joseph. *A Teaching Subject: Composition Since 1966.* Upper Saddle River, NJ: Prentice Hall, 1997.

Hartzog, Carol P. *Composition and the Academy: A Study of Writing Program Administration.* New York: MLA, 1986.

Hawkins, Thom. "Introduction." Olson vii-ix.

Heckathorn, Amy. "Moving toward a Group Identity: WPA Professionalization from the 1940s to the 1970s." *Historical Studies of Writing Program Administration: Individuals, Communities, and the Formation of a Discipline.* Ed. Barbara L'Eplattenier and Lisa Mastrangelo. West Lafayette: Parlor P, 2004. 191–219.

Heller, Adele, and Lois Rudnick. *1915: The Cultural Moment.* New Brunswick: Rutgers UP, 1991.

Herrington, Anne, and Charles Moran, eds. *Writing, Teaching, and Learning in the Disciplines.* New York: MLA, 1992.

Heyns, Roger W. "Divisiveness." *Educational Record* 58.1 (Winter 1977): 4–7.

Hirsch, E. D. *The Aims of Interpretation.* Chicago: U of Chicago P, 1976.

—. *The Philosophy of Composition.* Chicago: U of Chicago P, 1977.

—. *Validity in Interpretation.* New Haven: Yale UP, 1967.

Hollis, Karyn. "Autobiographical Writing at the Bryn Mawr School for Women Workers." *College Composition and Communication* 45 (1994): 31–60.

—. "Material of Desire: Bodily Rhetoric in Working Women's Poetry at the Bryn Mawr Summer School, 1921–1938." *Rhetorical Bodies.* Ed. Jack Selzer and Sharon Crowley. Madison: U of Wisconsin P, 1999. 98–119.

Horner, Winifred. "The Graduate Student Teacher-Training Program at the University of Missouri, Columbia." Neel 57–62.

Houp, Kenneth, and Thomas Pearsall. *Reporting Technical Information.* 3rd ed.. Beverly Hills: Glencoe P, 1977.

Howe, Harold III. "The Value of College: A Non-Economist's View" *Educational Record* 57.1 (Winter 1976): 5–12.

Hoy, John C. "Consumer Interest in Higher Education." *Educational Record.* 58.2 (Spring 1977): 180–90.

Hull, Glynda A., and David J. Bartholomae. "Basic Writing." Moran and Lunsford 265–302.

Hunt, Kellogg. *Grammatical Structures Written at Three Grade Levels.* Urbana, IL: NCTE, 1965.

Irmscher, William. *The Holt Guide to English: A Contemporary Handbook of Rhetoric, Language & Literature.* 2nd ed. Fort Worth: Harcourt, 1976.

Johnson, Nan. *Nineteenth-Century Rhetoric in North America.* Carbondale: Southern Illinois UP, 1991.

Jordan, Jay. "Dell Hymes, Kenneth Burke's 'Identification,' and the Birth of Sociolinguistics." *Rhetoric Review* 24 (2005): 264–79.

Keith, William. "Burke for the Composition Class." *College Composition and Communication* 28 (1977): 348–51.

Kerek, Andrew, Donald Daiker, and Max Morenberg. "Sentence Combining and College Composition." *Perceptual and Motor Skills: Monograph Supplement* 51 (1980): 1059–1157.

Kinneavy, James. *A Theory of Discourse: The Aims of Discourse.* New York: Norton, 1971.

—. "The Freshman Composition Program at the University of Texas at Austin." Neel 40–45.

—. "Writing Across the Curriculum." *ADE Bulletin* 76 (1983): 14–20.

Kneupper, Charles. "Dramatistic Invention: The Pentad as a Heuristic Procedure." *Rhetoric Society Quarterly* 9 (1979): 130–35.

—. "Teaching Argument: An Introduction to the Toulmin Model." *College Composition and Communication* 29 (October 1978): 237–41.

Labov, William. *Language in the Inner City.* Philadelphia: U of Pennsylvania P, 1972.

Lane, Frederick S. Rev. of *The End of Education: The Experience of the City University of New York with Open Enrollment and the Threat to Higher Education in America,* by Geoffrey Wagner. *Journal of Higher Education* 49 (1978): 529–30.

Lauer, Janice. "Constructing a Doctoral Program in Rhetoric and Composition." *Rhetoric Review* 12 (1994): 392–97.

—. "Disciplinary Formation: The Summer Rhetoric Seminar." *JAC* 18.3 (1998): 503-8.

—. "The Feminization of Rhetoric?" *Rhetoric Review* 13 (1995): 276–86.

—. "Getting to Know Rhetorica." Roen, Brown, and Enos. 57–82.

Leitch, Vincent B. *American Literary Criticism from the Thirties to the Eighties.* New York: Columbia UP, 1988.

L'Eplattenier, Barbara. "Finding Ourselves in the Past: An Argument for Historical Work on WPAs." Rose and Weiser 131–40.

L'Eplattenier, Barbara and Lisa Mastrangelo, eds. *Historical Studies of Writing Program Administration: Individuals, Communities, and the Formation of a Discipline.* West Lafayette, IN: Parlor P, 2004.

Leslie, David, Samuel E. Kellams, and C. Manny Gunne. *Part-Time Faculty in American Higher Education.* New York: Praeger, 1982.

Lester, Richard A. "The Fallacies of Numerical Goals." *Educational Record* 57.1 (Winter 1976): 58–64.

Lloyd-Jones, Richard. "The Politics of Research into the Teaching of Composition." *College Composition and Communication* 28 (1977): 218–22.

Lunsford, Andrea. "An Historical, Descriptive, and Evaluative Study of Remedial English in American Colleges and Universities." Diss. Ohio State U, 1977.

—. "Cognitive Development and Basic Writing." *College English* 41 (1979): 38–46.

Luthy, Melvin J. "Why Transformational Grammar Fails in the Classroom," *College Composition and Communication* 28 (1977): 352–55.

Macrorie, Ken. *Telling Writing.* New York: Hayden, 1970.

—. *The Vulnerable Teacher.* New York: Hayden, 1974.

Maimon, Elaine. "Writing Across the Curriculum: Past, Present, and Future." Griffin 67–74.

Maimon, Elaine, et al. *Writing in the Arts and Sciences.* Cambridge, MA: Winthrop, 1981.

Manning, Sylvia. "The Freshman Writing Program at the University of Southern California." Neel 79–83.

Martin, Cleo. "The Rhetoric Program at the University of Iowa." Neel 70–77.

Mathes, J. C., and Dwight Stevenson. *Designing Technical Reports: Writing for Audiences in Organizations.* Indianapolis: Bobbs-Merrill, 1976.

McCrimmon, James. *Writing with a Purpose.* 8th ed. Boston: Houghton, 1984.

McKeon, Richard. "Criticism and the Liberal Arts: The Chicago School of Criticism." *Profession 82.* Ed. Richard Brod and Phyllis Franklin. New York: MLA, 1982. 1–19.

McLeod, Susan H., and Margot Soven, eds. *Writing Across the Curriculum: A Guide to Developing Programs.* Newbury Park, CA: Sage, 1992.

McPherson, Elisabeth. Letter to the Editor. *Newsweek* 5 Jan. 1976: 4.

McQuade, Donald. "The Writing Program at Queens College of the City University of New York." Neel 16–23.

McQuade, Donald, ed. *Linguistics, Stylistics, and the Teaching of Composition.* Akron: U of Akron P, 1975.

Mellon, John C. *Transformational Sentence Combining: A Method for Enhancing the Development of Syntactic Fluency in College Composition.* Urbana: NCTE, 1969.

Meskin, Leslie, and Ronald B. Parker, Jr. "Who Says Johnny Can't Write?" *English Journal* 65.8 (1976): 42–46.

Miller, Susan. "Freshman English at Ohio State University." Neel 52–6.

—. *Textual Carnivals: The Politics of Composition.* Carbondale: Southern Illinois UP, 1991.

Miller, Thomas. *The Formation of College English.* Pittsburgh: U of Pittsburgh P, 1997.

—. "Teaching the Histories of a Rhetoric as Social Praxis." *Rhetoric Review* 12.1 (Fall 1993): 70–82.

Mills, Gordon, and John Walter. *Technical Writing.* 3rd ed. New York: Holt, Rinehart, and Winston, 1970.

Mirtz, Ruth M. "WPAs as Historians: Discovering a First-Year Writing Program by Researching Its Past." Rose and Weiser 119–30.

Moffett, James. *Teaching the Universe of Discourse.* Boston: Houghton, 1968.

Moran, Michael, and Ronald F. Lunsford, eds. *Research in Composition and Rhetoric: A Bibliographic Sourcebook.* Westport, CT: Greenwood P, 1984.

Morstain, Barry R., and Jerry G. Gaff. "Student Views of Teaching Improvements." *Educational Record* 58.3 (Summer 1977): 299–308.

Moye, Alfred L. "Meeting Student Demands: An Example of Voluntary Response." *Educational Record* 58.2 (Spring 1977): 191–200.

Munday, Leo A. "College Access for Nontraditional Students." *Journal of Higher Education* 47 (1976): 681–99.

Murphy, James J. "Rhetoric Studies Twenty-Five Years Ago and the Origins of ASHR." *Advances in the History of Rhetoric.* Vol. 6. Ed. Richard Leo Enos. Fort Worth: Texas Christian University, 2002. 2.

Murphy, Herta, and Charles Peck. *Effective Business Communications.* 2nd ed. New York: McGraw-Hill, 1976.

Murray, Donald. "Writing As Process: How Writing Finds Its Own Meaning." *Eight Approaches to Teaching Composition.* Ed. Timothy Donovan and Ben McClelland. Urbana: NCTE, 1980. 3–20.

—. "Write Before Writing." *College Composition and Communication* 29 (1978): 375–81.

National Center for Education Statistics. *Digest of Education Statistics.* Washington, D.C.: U.S. Dept. of Education, Office of Educational Research and Improvement, National Center for Education Statistics, 1989.

Neel, Jasper, ed. *Options for the Teaching of English: Freshman Composition.* New York: MLA, 1978.

Neel, Jasper, and Nelson, Jeanne C. "Doctoral Degrees Awarded in English, 1977–78: The MLA Placement Survey." *Profession 79.* Ed. Richard I. Brod and Jasper C. Neel. New York: MLA, 1979. 51–53.

North, Michael. *Reading 1922.* New York: Oxford UP, 2000.

O'Hare, Frank. *Sentence Combining: Improving Student Writing Without Formal Grammar Instruction.* Urbana: NCTE, 1973.

Ohmann, Richard. *English in America: A Radical View of the Profession.* New York: Oxford UP, 1976.

Olson, Gary A., ed. *Writing Centers: Theory and Administration.* Urbana: NCTE, 1984.

Ong, Walter. "The Writer's Audience Is Always a Fiction." *PMLA* 90 (1975): 9–21.

—. *Interfaces of the Word.* Ithaca: Cornell UP, 1977.

Parks, Stephen J. "A History of 'The Students' Right to Their Own Language' Resolution as Promulgated by the Conference on College Composition and Communication in 1974." Diss, University of Pittsburgh, 1985.

Pearsall, Thomas. *Teaching Technical Writing Methods for College English Teachers.* Washington, DC: Soc. for Technical Communication, 1975.

Pearsall, Thomas, and Thomas Warren. "The Council for Programs in Technical and Scientific Communication: A Retrospective." *Journal of Technical Writing and Communication* 26 (1996): 139–46.

Perelman, Chaim, and Lucie Olbrechts-Tyteca. *The New Rhetoric: A Treatise on Argument.* Notre Dame, IN: U of Notre Dame P, 1969.

Perelman, Chaim. *The Realm of Rhetoric.* Notre Dame, IN: U of Notre Dame P, 1982.

Poulakos, Takis, ed. *Rethinking the History of Rhetoric.* Boulder: Westview, 1993.

Ransom, John Crowe. *The New Criticism.* Norfolk, CT: New Directions, 1941.

Reager, A. Simone. "The State of the Humanities." *Educational Record* 59.2 (Spring 1978): 148–55.

Report of the Conference on College Freshman Courses in Composition and Communication Sponsored by the National Council of Teachers of English, Chicago, Illinois, April 1 and 2, 1949. Chicago: NCTE, n.d.

Roen, Duane, Stuart Brown, and Theresa Enos, eds. *Living Rhetoric and Composition: Stories of the Discipline.* Mahwah, NJ: Erlbaum, 1999.

Rohman, Gordon, and Albert Wlecke. *The Construction and Application of Models for Concept Formation.* East Lansing, MI: Health, Education, and Welfare Cooperative Research Project #2174, 1964.

Rohter, Larry, and Tom Zito. "Rock Idol Elvis Presley Dies at 42." *Washington Post* 17 Aug. 1977: A3.

Rose, Shirley K. "Preserving Our Histories of Institutional Change: Enabling Research in the Writing Program Archives." Rose and Weiser 107–18.

Rose, Shirley K, and Irwin Weiser, eds. *The Writing Program Administrator as Researcher.* Portsmouth, NH: Boynton/Cook, 1999.

Rubinstein, S. Leonard. "Composition: A Collision with Literature." *College English* 27 (1966): 273–77.

—. "Let Us Teach Writing as a Subject." *AAHE Bulletin* (Dec. 1982): 5–7.

—. *Writing: A Habit of Mind.* New York: William C. Brown, 1972.

Russell, David R. "American Origins of the Writing-Across-the-Curriculum Movement." Herrington and Moran 22–44.

—. "Writing Across the Curriculum in Historical Perspective: Toward a Social Interpretation." *College English* 52 (1990): 53–73.

—. *Writing in the Academic Disciplines, 1870–1990: A Curricular History.* Carbondale: Southern Illinois UP, 1991.

Sams, Henry. "Writing." *The Idea and Practice of General Education, by Present and Former Members of the Faculty.* Chicago: U of Chicago P, 1950. 204–11.

Sawyer, Thomas, ed. *Technical and Professional Communication: Teaching in the Two-Year College, Four-Year College, and Professional School.* Ann Arbor: Professional Communication P, 1972.

Schaefer, William D. "Editor's Column." *PMLA* 93.5 (1978): 859–60.

Scott, Robert L. "Rhetoric As Epistemic Ten Years Later." *Central States Speech Journal* 27 (1976): 9–16.

Selzer, Jack. *Kenneth Burke in Greenwich Village: Conversing with the Moderns, 1915–1931.* Madison: U of Wisconsin P, 1996.

Shaughnessy, Mina P. "Basic Writing." Tate 177-206.

—. "Diving In: An Introduction to Basic Writing." *College Composition and Communication* 27 (1976): 234–39.

—. *Errors and Expectations: A Guide for the Teacher of Basic Writing.* New York: Oxford UP, 1977.

Shor, Ira. "Our Apartheid: Writing Instruction and Inequality." *Journal of Basic Writing* 16 (1997): 91–103.

Simmons, Sue Carter. "Constructing Writers: Barrett Wendell's Pedagogy at Harvard." *College Composition and Communication* 46 (1995): 327–52.

Sledd, James. "Bi-Dialecticalism: The Linguistics of White Supremacy." *English Journal* 58 (1969): 1307–15; 1329. Rpt. in Freed 31–44.

—. "English for Survival." *The English Record* 26 (1975): 11–21. Rpt. in Freed 70–81.

—. "Return to Service." Paper given at the Penn State Conference on Rhetoric and Composition: Rhetorical Education in America, State College, PA. 6 July 1999.

Smith, Mary Ann. "The National Writing Project after Twenty-Two Years." *Phi Delta Kappan* 77 (June 1996): 688–92.

Smitherman, Geneva. "CCCC's Role in the Struggle for Language Rights." *College Composition and Communication* 50 (1999): 349–76.

—. *Talkin' and Testifyin'*. Detroit: Wayne State UP, 1977.

Solomon, Henry, ed. "The Growing Influence of Federal Regulations." *Educational Record* 57.3 (Summer 1977): 270–89.

Souther, James. *Technical Report Writing.* Melbourne: Krieger, 1984.

—. "Teaching Technical Writing: A Retrospective Appraisal." *Technical Writing: Theory and Practice.* Ed. Bertie E. Fearing and W. Keats Sparrow. New York: MLA, 1989. 2–13.

Staples, Katherine. "Technical Communication from 1950 to 1998: Where Are We Now?" *Technical Communication Quarterly* 8 (1999): 153–64.

Steele, Claude M., and Stephen G. Green. "Affirmative Action and Academic Hiring: A Case Study of a Value Conflict." *The Journal of Higher Education* 47 (1976): 413–35.

Steinmann, Martin, ed. *The New Rhetorics.* New York: Charles Scribner's Sons, 1967.

Stewart, Donald. *The Authentic Voice: A Pre-Writing Approach to Student Writing.* Dubuque, IA: W. C. Brown Co., 1972

—. "Composition Textbooks and the Assault on Tradition." *College Composition and Communication* 29 (1978): 171–76.

Stoen, Don. "Stuttering Pencils." *English Journal* 65.8 (1976): 40–41.

Strain, Margaret. "Local Histories, Rhetorical Negotiations: The Development of Doctoral Programs in Rhetoric and Composition." *Rhetoric Society Quarterly* 30 (2000): 57–76.

Strong, William. *Sentence Combing: A Composing Book.* New York: Random, 1973.

Tate, Gary, ed. *Teaching Composition: Ten Bibliographic Essays.* Fort Worth: Texas UP, 1976.

Tibbetts, A. M. "On the Practical Uses of a Grammatical System: A Note on Christensen and Johnson." *Rhetoric and Composition: A Sourcebook for Teachers.* Ed. Richard Graves. Rochelle Park, NJ: Hayden, 1976. 139–49.

Tompkins, Jane, ed. *Reader-Response Criticism: From Formalism to Post-Structuralism.* Baltimore: Johns Hopkins UP, 1980.

Toulmin, Stephen. *The Uses of Argument.* Cambridge: Cambridge UP, 1964.

Toulmin, Stephen, Richard Rieke, and Allan Janik. *An Introduction to Reasoning.* New York: Macmillan, 1979.

VanDeWeghe, Robert. "Research in Composition and the Design of Writing Programs" *ADE Bulletin* 61 (May 1979): 28–31.

Varnum, Robin. *Fencing with Words: A History of Writing Instruction at Amherst College During the Era of Theodore Baird, 1938–1966.* Urbana, IL: NCTE, 1996.

Veit, Richard. "Are Machines the Answer?" *Writing Lab Newsletter* 4 (1979): 1–2.

Vitanza, Victor. "Retrospective/Prospective." *PRE/TEXT: The First Decade.* Ed. Victor Vitanza. Pittsburgh: U of Pittsburgh P, 1993. xi-xxiii.

—. *Writing Histories of Rhetoric.* Carbondale: Southern Illinois UP, 1994.

Wagner, Geoffrey. *The End of Education. The Experience of the City University of New York with Open Enrollment and the Threat to Higher Education in America.* Cranbury, NJ: A.S. Barnes, 1976.

Walshe, R. D. "A Model of the Writing Situation." *College Composition and Communication* 28 (1977): 384–86.

Warnock, John. "New Rhetoric and the Grammar of Pedagogy." *Freshman English News* 5.2 (Fall 1976): 1–22.

—. "William Coles." *Encyclopedia of Rhetoric and Composition.* Ed. Theresa Enos. New York: Garland, 1996. 113.

Warnock, John, and Tilly [Eggers] Warnock. "The Freshman Writing Program at the University of Wyoming." Neel 1–9.

Weaver, Richard. *Ideas Have Consequences.* Chicago: U of Chicago P, 1948.

—. *Language Is Sermonic.* Baton Rouge: Louisiana State UP, 1970.

Weaver, Robert, and Patricia Weaver. *Persuasive Writing: A Manager's Guide to Effective Letters and Reports.* New York: Free Press, 1977.

Weeks, Francis. "The Teaching of Business Writing at the Collegiate Level, 1900–1920." *Studies in the History of Business Writing.* Ed. George H. Douglas and Herbert W. Hildebrandt. Urbana: American Business Communication Assoc., 1985. 201–15.

Wellek, Rene. "The New Criticism: Pros and Cons." *Critical Inquiry* 4 (1978): 611–24.

Wellek, Rene, and Austin Warren. *Theory of Literature.* New York: Harcourt, 1942

Wells, Walter. *Communications in Business.* 2nd edition. Belmont, CA: Wadsworth, 1977.

Wergin, Jon F., Elizabeth J. Mason, and Paul J. Munson. "The Practice of Faculty Development." *Journal of Higher Education* 47 (1976): 289–308.

"Why Johnny Can't Write." *Newsweek* 8 Dec. 1975: 58–62.

Wiener, Harvey. *The Writing Room: A Resource Book for Teachers of English.* New York: Oxford UP, 1981.

Williams, Joseph. "Non-Linguistic Linguistics and the Teaching of Style." *Language: Journal of the Linguistic Society of America* 52 (1976): 461–78.

—. *The New English.* New York: Free Press, 1970.

Winterowd, W. Ross. *The Contemporary Writer: A Practical Rhetoric.* Fort Worth: Harcourt, 1975.

—. *The English Department: A Personal and Institutional History.* Carbondale: Southern Illinois UP, 1998.

—. "The Grammar of Coherence." *Contemporary Rhetoric: A Conceptual Background with Readings.* Ed. W. Ross Winterowd. New York: Harcourt, 1975. 225–32.

"Writing Projects." *The Arizona English Bulletin* 22 (1980).

Young, Richard. "Paradigms and Problems: Needed Research in Rhetorical Invention." *Research on Composing: Points of Departure.* Ed. Charles Cooper and Lee Odell. Urbana: NCTE, 1978. 29–47.

Young, Richard, Alton Becker, and Kenneth Pike. *Rhetoric: Discovery and Change.* New York: Harcourt, 1970.

Index